I AM A

WOMAN

FINDING

MY *VOICE*

EAGLE BROOK
William Morrow
and Company, Inc.
New York

I AM A
*W*OMAN
FINDING
MY *V*OICE

~

*C*elebrating
the Extraordinary Blessings
of Being a Woman

JANET F. QUINN, PH.D., R.N.

Published by Eagle Brook

An Imprint of William Morrow and Company, Inc.

1350 Avenue of the Americas, New York, N.Y. 10019

It is the policy of William Morrow and Company, Inc., and its imprints and affiliates,
recognizing the importance of preserving what has been written, to print the books
we publish on acid-free paper, and we exert our best efforts to that end.

Library of Congress Cataloging-in-Publication Data

Quinn, Janet F.

I am a woman finding my voice   :   celebrating the extraordinary

blessings of being a woman / by Janet F. Quinn. —1st ed.

p.   cm.

ISBN 0-688-16743-8

1. Women—Psychology—Miscellanea.   2. Women—Social conditions—

Miscellanea.   3. Affirmations.   I. Title.

HQ1206.Q56   1999

305.42—dc21   98-49835

CIP

Printed in the United States of America

First Edition

2 3 4 5 6 7 8 9 10

BOOK DESIGN BY DEBORAH KERNER

www.williammorrow.com

FOR ALL WOMEN, EVERY WOMAN,
*may you know your awesome goodness and
celebrate the abundant gifts that your life bestows on a needy world.*

IN MEMORY OF MY MOTHER, GEORGIANNA SWEET QUINN,
*in whose arms I first knew unconditional love
and whose touch I miss still.*

FOR MY SISTER, DIANE QUINN COLEMAN,
*with my deepest wishes for your healing,
wholeness, and peace.*

FOR TARA MICHELLE AND FAITH MARIE,
*with all my love and prayers that your lives as women
are radiant with boundless love, joy, and beauty.*

FOR THE EAGLE,
*in all its manifestations in my life.
Here, I can only fall silent.*

CONTENTS

$\mathcal{F}$OREWORD

by Dr. Joan Borysenko

$\mathcal{A}$ foreword is supposed to be a clever piece of writing, an enticing doorway that beckons you into the heart of a book. It is meant to encourage you to take time for yourself and to enter an enchanted world where treasures await. I find myself humbled by this task, searching for words to do this honest, poetic, wise book justice. Janet, the author, is also a dear and precious friend. I want to write something that honors all she has meant to me and to the many people all around the world who have been touched and inspired by her lectures and retreats.

As I read Janet's stories and affirmations, I responded with the aahs and mmms that are a woman's spontaneous and embodied form of saying amen. I have felt that way, too. I know the truth of that experience in my bones, and it gives me gooseflesh. And as a friend of mine once quipped, you can fake an orgasm, but you can't fake gooseflesh. Nor can you fake the tears and laughter that will surely be your companions as you see yourself in Janet's stories, reclaiming bits and pieces of your own experience through hers. For this is how we women serve one another, mirroring experiences and weaving wisdom from our mutual reflections.

Like Janet, I spent most of my adult life as an academic in a male world. I tried to learn how to act like a man in that venue and I was reasonably successful. I made a point of saying that I had never experienced any discrimination as a woman, that life was what you made of it. I was right. I made myself a man and lost sympathy with both other women and with my own feminine nature. But at midlife there was a calling from the disowned part of myself. I defected from academia and began the slow process of discovering what it was to be a woman. In the spirit of teaching what you need to learn, I began to cofacilitate women's spiritual retreats. One of life's special pleasures is to have facilitated some of those retreats with Janet. Through the women, in both prayerful silence and spirited conversation, I have learned to cherish the gift of my female birth.

I can recognize myself and other friends in Janet's stories, recalling the times we shared that became the precious body of friendship. In reading her essay on how women are there for each other—for things like breast biopsies—a memory surfaces. I was the biopsied buddy whom Janet and another friend of ours, Jan, was there for. I had recently been divorced and was living by myself on a wild mountaintop, and these women were like angels coming to my aid. Throwing caution to the wind, Janet drove up the mountain, three thousand vertical feet above her home in Boulder, in the dead of winter after a big snowfall to bring me to the hospital. Janet doesn't like driving in snow and doesn't have a four-wheel-drive vehicle, but she insisted on coming anyhow. She took a wrong turn and got stuck in a snowdrift. As I drove myself down to the hospital I was consumed with anguish. What if Janet had gone over a cliff?

Our friend Jan was there when I got to the hospital and stayed with me through the biopsy. Such a comfort she was. Janet arrived as the procedure was being completed and insisted on coming back home with me and staying the night. I was in high spirits because the magnification studies suggested that the problem was benign. So Janet and I went to the gourmet grocery and the video store. We were planning a celebratory evening. But when I walked in the door and took off my jacket, it seemed heavy and it was dripping—not with snow, it turned out, but with blood.

I had probably lost a pint already and was delighted that my good friend happened to be a nurse. Janet laid me out and applied direct pressure to the small artery that had been nicked during the biopsy. She called the hospital, spoke to the doctor. Neither of us wanted to go down the mountain again in the deepening snow unless there was no choice. So she sat there with her thumb in the dike, stemming the tide of my blood. It took almost four hours for the bleeding to stop, just as our friend Jan, a physician, arrived with her medical kit. Thank God they were there and that an experience that might have been frightening was, instead, the ground out of which a deeper friendship grew.

My hope and prayer is that this book will be a friend for you, inviting you more deeply into who you are, celebrating your victories, reminding you of the wisdom in your mistakes, bringing a smile of knowing to your lips. This is a book that you will keep and cherish, reading and rereading often as you change through the days and years. This is a book that you can give to your mother, sisters, and friends. It is a gift of the heart for your daughters, nieces, students, and godchildren. It is a book to savor alone and to read to one another. Janet has invited you into her world. It is one rich with love and wisdom, and I am ever so grateful to have joined her in it.

$\mathcal{P}$REFACE

$\mathcal{I}$ have used the phrase *I am a woman* as the stem for the meditations in this book. When it began several years ago as a slim pamphlet, the book was a collection of affirmations I had written for myself at a time when I needed to be reminded of who I was and what I was trying to do. I inscribed the affirmations into small stones made from polymer clay. I would select one stone and carry it with me throughout the day to help me remember. This book is larger and broader in scope and purpose than the little book of affirmations. Yet I still need to be reminded of who I am and what I am trying to do and to celebrate who I have become. I thought that other women might appreciate these reminders, too, so I continued writing with the same stem, grounding each meditation in the basic truth of our lives—*we are women*.

You can open the book and start reading anywhere, although I suggest beginning with the introduction. You might want to use the meditations as I do—as affirmations to carry with you throughout the day—for while the stories are mine, if they contain any truths, those truths belong to all of us. However you decide to approach this book, I feel privileged to share it with you. I hope that it inspires you to find your own voice as a woman and to share that voice with the world. Please don't miss the pages at the end of this book, which you can use for writing your own meditations and reflections.

—JANET FRANCES QUINN
Boulder, Colorado

ACKNOWLEDGMENTS

$\mathcal{T}$his book would never have been birthed without the vision and guidance of my editor and my agents. Joann Davis, my editor at Eagle Brook, has made this, my first book-writing experience, a joy from start to finish. It is she who saw in me and my work the potential for this kind of writing before I even knew that it was where I wanted to go. I do not know how she did it. I only know that she did. She invited me out from behind my academic persona to find another voice, my own voice, and then supported me in doing it. Truly, I have never felt so nurtured and affirmed by critique and suggestion, so respected in editorial revising. Joann, you have been an extraordinary blessing to me. My deepest gratitude goes to you.

My agents, Madeleine Morel and Barbara Lowenstein, quite literally made this project happen for me. They, too, saw something which I was only beginning to see in myself and helped me to develop it. Both were relentless at times in encouraging me to persist. I'm so glad they did! Thank you both.

My friends are like a net that holds me up, a circle around me forming a web of interconnections that sustain me. I speak to some of these friends only rarely, yet their presence in my life continues to orient me, grounding me in my own history and strengthening me in memory and in our occasional contacts. Lillie Burnette; Wayne Cavalier; Sylvia Fabriani; Priya Hanson; Patricia Hopkins; Cynthia Hutchinson; Charlotte Kerr; John Laird; Wayne Muller; Karen Peters; Marilyn Schlitz; Dale Schroedel; Gary Schwartz; and Carol Wells-Federman—thank you so much for calling me friend and maintaining a grip on me even when I disappear. Truly, you provide one of the greatest miracles of my life—undeserved, unconditional love.

Eloise Monzillo and Patricia Moccia have been through most of the trials and triumphs of my adult life with me—and I with them. Thank you for all the years of ongoing love and support. Patricia— I think we did it! And Roseanne (Pooper) Torpey—you are in a class all your own—as always! Thanks for birthday cards, chocolate bunnies at Easter, and laughter anytime!

Chuck Barr has contributed more than I can say to helping me grow into the person I most want to be. Thanks, Chuck, for continuing to be a loving, supportive presence in my life, and for all the ways you keep me from self-destructing through my maintenance deficiencies. Thanks, too, for encouraging me to write. Thanks to Denny Webster for creating rituals for us to get together, sharing our lives, present and future, and to Phyllis Klaif for the sweetest and most undemanding affection. My youngest brother, Bill, is better than any other Quinn at staying in touch—thanks, Bill, for your caring and concern.

Wendy Trafford McKenna, Chuck McKenna, and Faith Marie, my heart is yours. Thank you for making me a godmother again and for welcoming me into your family. I truly feel as if I belong there, and this is a source of deep joy that sustains me in some of the dry times.

To Jean Watson, I give thanks for the inspiration and wisdom you share with me and with the world. As we have journeyed together, particularly over these last months, I have seen the truth that the human spirit really can bear the unbearable and still walk in beauty and light, seeking to give itself away. Thank you for the teachings and for allowing me to walk with you. It has been my great privilege.

I am grateful to my writing group—Joan Borysenko, Judith

Gass, Amina Knowlen, Lynnea Lombard, and Jan Shepherd—for providing the vehicle for me to begin exploring in earnest my potential as a writer. More than that, it gave me the opportunity to get to know Joan and Jan, who have become irreplaceable to me. Thank you both for standing with me in my place of "don't know" and never once giving up on me. Thank you for taking each of my attempts to step out of it seriously and for honoring me still when it became clear that the step was only a circle-turn back in. Joan, your generosity of Spirit, openhearted goodness, and wild and crazy womanself are food for my soul. Working with you is a joyful and effortless dance, and I love that we help people to touch God, together. Thank you so much for your friendship and for all your help in making this book possible. Jan, I do not know how I could have done this without your support and your love. Thanks for reading and responding to drafts of this book, but most of all thanks for believing in me from the beginning and for loving me no matter what. To Dick Behler, thanks for sharing Jan with me and for becoming a friend and support in your own right. The Rio Trio has a date when this book is published!

I want to thank TM, who is my hero. You changed my life in one, holy, caring moment. You let me know that there really are White Knights disguised as ordinary men and you gave me hope for humanity and for my own future when I was nearly out of both. And last but not least, you are the only person I know who realizes what a french fry really is! I hope you will see in this book some of the fruits of your gifts to me—and that they will give you joy.

Finally, I must thank all of the friends, students, colleagues, patients, workshop participants, and retreatants who have, over the years, called forth from me my best self and who have given me back my deepest knowing. My thanks and love to each of you, and my wishes for your continuing growth, renewal, and joy.

$\mathcal{I}$NTRODUCTION

We sat in a small circle of women on the reddest earth I have ever seen. There had been a recent rain, and the new desert growth was so brilliantly green and shiny that it looked almost plastic. Some of us played the musical sticks, hitting them together in time with the clapping of the old ones as they sang a song of beginning. The sticks are hand carved by the men, then elaborately decorated by the women as they all sit together around the central fire singing. The wood itself is mulgar, which is plentiful in that desert and which has an unforgettable, pungent smell that is released with the warmth of one's hands or as it burns in the fire. Sometimes still I hold those sticks until the aroma gives itself up to me and I remember.

The singing quieted, and Nganyinytja, the Aboriginal elder who had invited us to her *place* in the heart of the Australian outback, spoke through the translator. Her fingers never stopped drawing in the soft, silky dirt, illustrating her words with symbols and images. "We will talk now of women's business. This business belongs only to the women. Women must never speak of this business to men or when men are present. The men have men's business and will not speak of it to the women."

I was quick to respond. I asked the translator to query Nganyinytja about which is more important, women's business or men's business. Our teacher looked at me curiously. She shook her head slowly back and forth, and I assumed that she had not understood the question, so I asked it in a different way. Which has more status in the tribe, I wanted to know, men's business or women's business? I was, of course, assuming that I already knew the answer.

The translator once again queried our teacher. Nganyinytja again shook her head back and forth and finally spoke, drawing a circle in the sand and moving her fingers around it, over and over, deepening it with each pass. Diana translated. "She says she understands your words, but your question makes no sense. There is no business which is more important than any other. All business, women's business, men's business, is needed for the sake of the whole. All the work must be done; it is all important to the whole tribe."

Nganyinytja looked away, paused, and then began our lessons in women's business. And while all of these teachings were meaningful to me, the first teaching I received from Nganyinytja will always be the most powerful. In that one moment, hundreds and hundreds of miles from any form of modern life and thousands of miles from my civilized, politically correct, academic world, I had been given a new understanding of feminism. I have never been the same.

This book is a celebration of the feminine soul. Perhaps it is still not politically correct to speak of such a thing as a uniquely feminine soul, but in finding my own voice, I must speak of it anyway. The feminism of the 1960s and 1970s was a critical step in the achievement of equality for women. We fought for equal pay for equal work; equal opportunities for education and employment; and the right to choose whether we would marry or not, have children or not, stay at home or not. These battles needed to be fought, positions needed to be articulated, laws needed to be created. As a woman who came of age during the women's movement, I have both contributed to and benefited from the advancements that have been made in women's rights. It had to happen, and maybe it happened the only way it could.

But somehow, here at midlife in the late 1990s, it seems to me that we may have lost something at least as valuable as the rights we gained. Somehow we decided that to be equal to men meant we needed to be the same as men. Somehow we decided that to be heard, we had to speak in men's voices; to be seen, we had to wear men's clothes; to count, we had to do men's jobs. Off we went, a whole generation of women, into every facet of American work life, with our double-breasted suits and hardhats, briefcases and lunch pails. Whatever they could do, we could do, maybe even better. And certainly whatever we had been doing, we didn't have to do anymore.

Yet as a friend said recently, a lot got lost in the pinstripes. Somehow in the process we lost our own authentic voice, the voice of the deep feminine soul, and settled for a genderless, neutered equality. This book represents an attempt to regain that voice in all its dimensions, to reconnect with what it means to be a woman, and to celebrate it with joy and passion. For as Nganyinytja taught us, we need "all the business" for the good of the whole. It does not serve us or our world to value one voice more than the other, the masculine more than the feminine, men's business more than women's business. Nor does it serve us any longer to keep denying that men and women are, well, different. The world needs all the tender, loving, caring feminine energy women can give it, not instead of our power and our strength, but served by them.

Finding our voice as women is not a matter of picking out one note and singing it for life; it is not as simplistic an idea as the reduction of women to some predetermined list of traits or qualities. Women's voice is far more like an orchestra than a single instrument; more like a complex harmony than a single chord. Finding our voice is discovering all of the notes that comprise our deepest selves and claiming our right to express them as the song which is uniquely ours to sing. This song may be different every day, because we are different every day, and so finding our voice is about being free to change our tune without being labeled weak-minded or criticized for being fickle. Finding our voice is about allowing the full volume and tonal quality of our whole beings to be expressed; it's about the liberty to compose a unique and personal rendition of the essential womanliness that is expressing itself through each of us.

Most of all, above all, beyond all, is this: A woman who has found her full voice, who can express the symphony of her heart's passion, her soul's wisdom, her body's phenomenal strength and beauty, and her mind's knowing is a woman who is free to be fully who she was born to be. As long as there are notes and chords and melodies of experience within us that we disown, or that we remain fearful of expressing, or that we are prevented from expressing, we are not free.

This freedom matters mightily, not just to the individual woman but to all women, to all beings, because we are not separate from one another. When one woman becomes more free, all women become more free. And as more and more women become free, there is more freedom for the feminine energies, the energies of relationship and connection, to pour forth on a world that desperately needs more, not less of this essential stuff.

When we find our own, authentic voice as women, we use our power to nurture life, love, relationship, and community, not corporate takeovers and the accumulation of wealth. We become unafraid of sounding weak when we are speaking *just like a woman;* we refuse to be embarrassed when we use our hard-earned freedom to pursue our feminine visions of a world in which love really does matter—it does, you know, it matters the very most.

When we recover our full song we come to a new place of understanding that we do not, and never did, belong only to ourselves.

We recognize that all our hard work, the painful, tediously hard work of giving birth to ourselves and becoming whole was for only one purpose. It is not simply to become *the best that we can be*—that is a means, not an end. We become healed, whole, and free so that we may become instruments for Love itself; so that we can give ourselves away, pour ourselves out in the service of life, and be filled again, over and over in the infinite circle of love and care and connection that is the whole. This is not pathological; this is not dysfunctional; this is our birthright as women; this is the sound of singing ourselves home.

I AM A

Woman

FINDING

MY Voice

I Am a Woman

*M*y most fundamental truth is that I am a woman. From the moment I was conceived, I have been female; daughter of Creation; girl-child becoming woman; living, being, dying, woman. Working, playing, singing, loving, woman. It is the only thing that will never change. It is one thing that I know about myself finally and certainly. Why has this obvious truth escaped me for so long? Why have I spent so many years fighting to be thought of and treated as "a person" rather than valued and esteemed as a woman? Such a betrayal of my essence, this neutered equality. I am equal to, but not the same as, men—and I thank the Divine that it is so! I claim and celebrate my being, be-ing, in this world as WOMAN— with womanvalues and womanviews and womanrhythms and womanblood and womanheart and womansoul. *I am a woman.*

I Am a Woman Finding My Voice

*D*id I first lose my voice when I learned not to cry too loud or make too much noise so I didn't wake up Daddy? Or was it when I learned that talking in church was a sin (unless it was to a priest)? Was it the first time I didn't say what was inside of me because I didn't want to make someone mad, or was it the first time that I said what wasn't true because I didn't want to hurt someone's feelings? No matter now. Now, I am finding my voice! I am laughing, screaming, crying, and cooing! I am making delighted sounds and angry sounds. I growl and moan, and I sing and chant! I offer soft and sweet words of comfort and passion and I speak loud, clear words of outrage and opposition. I am making holy noise and I am keeping holy, holy silence. Finding my voice means that I claim my freedom to express myself. It means that I speak only what is true for me, and that I will never be silenced again. I am a ***woman finding my voice!***

I Am a Woman Healing Myself

*T*he word *heal* comes from the Anglo-Saxon *haelan,* which means to be or to become whole. To be a woman healing myself is to be a woman becoming whole; giving myself the time and the space I need for the journey. No one grows up without wounds—emotional wounds; spiritual wounds; psychological wounds. I may want to forget how I have been hurt, bury it and just move on, but sometimes my wounds keep me from becoming all that I want to be, and so I need to pay attention to them.

I am the first of five children. I was twenty-two months old when my brother was born. Then came a sister two years after that, then a brother, then another brother. With each addition, I became further removed from the nurturing lap of my mother and became more my mother's helper. This is so normal and usual that it hardly seems important to think about, let alone to present as a wound for healing. Yet this was when I learned that it wasn't a good idea to expect people to love me, because eventually they would need to give that love to someone else. Other people needed love more than I did. Better to let God love me, and to try to be a good little helper.

Healing is discovering all the secret places inside of me, especially the ones I feel ashamed of or frightened by, and befriending them. Healing is the process I am engaged in and not a specific outcome. I fill my life with people and things that nourish and feed me and I try to avoid anything that is not healing for me and anyone who does violence to my unfolding. I do not know what the outcome of this process will be, what my healing will look like, or feel like, even to myself, because healing is always creative. Yet I have come to trust that, no matter what it looks like, feels like, or sounds like, no matter how long it is taking, or how foreign the territory, I am a *woman healing myself*.

I Am a Woman Saying YES

*Y*ES! YES! *YES,* the word of affirmation, of opening, of movement and flow; the word that means *it is so.* YES, giving permission, allowing unfolding, clarity, and sureness—YES! Now, finally, I am saying YES! YES to all of me, all of the parts. YES to the light and loving and free parts. YES to the dark and angry and scared parts. YES to all of my feelings, the ones I like and the ones I don't like. YES to my tenderness and loving and nurturing. Yes to my wisdom and strength and courage. YES to my fears and longings and confusions. YES to my sexuality, my passion, and my responsiveness. YES to my longing to hold another; to join, to merge, to know ecstatic union. YES to my need for solitude, spiritual practice, and communion with God in nature. YES to walking as woman in this world; no hiding, no shame, no apologies. I stand tall and centered on the earth, reaching my arms upward and I become YES and I say YES to the unfolding mystery of my life. I am a ***woman saying YES.***

I Am a Woman Saying NO

*N*O! Such freedom in saying *NO!* A tiny word, prohibited for so long, forbidden to leave the lips of a good little girl or a sweet young woman. NO, carefully avoided by a professional on the career ladder who mustn't be accused of not being a team player. NO withheld in intimate relationships because NO is so selfish and so, well, negative. I do not know if it is age alone that has transformed my relationship to NO, but transformed it is.

Now I realize that saying YES without the possibility of saying NO is hollow and joyless. I know that YES without the possibility of NO is allowing myself to be taken from, rather than to freely give. YES without the possibility of NO is never the truth. More and more, I am claiming the fullness of my right to choose; I am celebrating my freedom to be a woman saying NO! NO to anything that is not true for me. NO to anything that diminishes me or reduces me to less than who I am. NO to anyone who would abuse my gentle and kind womanspirit or who would try to break my fierce and powerful womanspirit. NO to injustice, to violence, to hungry children, to keeping the secrets of oppressors. NO to ways of being in the world that come out of fear, impoverishment, anxiety, or the need to control or to please. NO to YES when I really mean NO! I am a *woman saying NO.*

I Am a Woman Re-claiming My Body

*M*y body, at last, I claim you! I live here! I am not some disincarnate spirit using just any vehicle to get around. I live in the full, round, soft, juicy, wet, strong, agile, capable, Spirit-filled, nurturing, graceful, flowing, comforting, lovely, smooth, dancing, singing, playing, working, praying body of a woman!

For so many years I rejected my body because it isn't perfect according to the standards of my culture. I have been unfaithful to it, letting other's opinions turn me against it, allowing others to use it without love, without tenderness. Because I myself rejected my body, I didn't protect it, didn't demand that it be treated like the precious gift that it is. My body, the temple of my soul, deserves better from me.

I re-claim this body. I re-claim these eyes and their vision; this mouth and its words; these arms and legs and their hugging and dancing. I re-claim these breasts and their magnificent fullness; I re-claim these wide, round hips and strong, fleshy thighs and their walking on the earth. I re-claim this vagina and all its secret folds and this womb and its bleeding. I re-claim all of my body's parts, named and unnamed. This body is a miracle; it is the first gift of the Creator to me—my birthday present. I take this body to have and to hold, in sickness and in health, to honor, love, and cherish until death do us part. I am a *woman re-claiming my body!*

A Reflection: On learning to love my body

*H*ow I have struggled to accept this body just the way it is! I reclaim it, marry it, divorce it. I make peace and then I make war again. But in the last several years, a new awareness has emerged that is helping me keep my vows to my body. What I have noticed is that the internal battle completely dissolves when I am using my body in ways that allow me to appreciate its power and strength and amazing capacity for pleasure and joy.

When I return from a jog, wet with sweat, panting, with a beet red face, I love my body. When my broken ankle healed all by itself—no instructions from me—I loved my body. When I walk on the mountain trails behind my house and see yucca plants flowering and oozing a slippery, shimmering juice and dozens of ladybugs feasting on the nectar, I love the body that got me there and the senses that are filled with delight. When I am lying in the arms of my beloved after making love, close and sweet and feeling so cared for, I love my body. When my godchild, Faith, was only days old, sound asleep nestled into my bosom as we lay together on the couch, I loved my body.

In each of these instances there is no separation between my body and me—it's just I, having an experience that I can have only in a body—moving, running, seeing, smelling, touching, tasting. What happens when I am hating my body size or shape is that I have separated myself from my body, I eye it as if it were some object utterly unrelated to me, a bag of flesh and bone (especially flesh), and then I judge it as not measuring up to some ideal I have in my mind. It's a fracturing, a splitting apart of body, mind, and soul.

So there it is. To love my body more, I need to allow myself to have more bodily pleasure. I don't need to wait until I am the perfect size. I can start now, today, by taking more lavender-scented bubble baths; going for more walks in nature; dancing around the living room more often; jogging for forty-five minutes instead of thirty; holding more babies; and *making more love. I may still choose to work on losing some extra weight or strengthening my muscles. But my work won't be about battering my body into a more acceptable size so I can then, presumably, have more pleasure in it. It will be about keeping this body, which already gives me so much pleasure, fit and strong so that my pleasure can last a lifetime and my embodiment can continue to serve the people and the work that I love for all of my days.*

I Am a Woman Telling Myself the Truth

*O*ther people can be my greatest source of freedom or the chains that I allow to ensnare me. When their ideas stimulate me to search for my own knowing, to stretch for a new comprehension of an old problem, or to venture forward in my own creativity, they are a pathway to freedom. But when I allow other people's ideas and beliefs to determine what I will allow myself to think, feel, do, be, or say, then I am participating in my own imprisonment. To be and continue to become my own true self, I must tell my own truth, at least to myself, even when it isn't politically correct or acceptable to the other people in my life. Because I want to know who I really am and what I really think and how I really feel, I am a *woman telling myself the truth.*

I Am a Woman Claiming My Wisdom

*T*here are things I know, things I have learned from deep in-side, from other women; from holding children; from look-ing into the eyes of dying patients and tending their bodies when life has departed; from living my life listening to the voice in the river or the wind, the caw of a crow, the stillness of deep night. There are things I know that will never be measured, that cannot be assigned numbers or analyzed under a microscope. They cannot be seen; will never be reproduced in exactly the same way and are utterly un-controlled. That, at last, is okay with me. I know these things. That is what I know. I am a *woman claiming my wisdom.*

I Am a Woman Believing in Myself

I believe in my strength and my resilience and my capacity to do hard things. I believe in my vision and my dreams and my ability to do whatever I choose to do. I believe in my very bright mind, my loving heart, and my womansoul. I believe in the clarity of my perceptions and the astuteness of my insights. I believe in my knowing and the depth of all that life has taught me. I believe in my willingness to wait and to perceive the right time for action and the right time for letting go. I believe in my openness to my own and other's pain, facing it with neither denial nor indulgence but with grace and fortitude and even acceptance. I believe that I can survive just about anything that life asks of me if I remember that I am a child of God, made in her image and held in her love. I am a *woman believing in myself.*

I Am a Woman Loving Myself

*H*ow many times and for how many years I have looked into the eyes of another—friends, lovers, even strangers—asking, "Will you love me?" Yet no one can give me what I have not given myself. I cannot replace self-love with the love of others because, unless I love myself, I can't take in the gift. That's the paradox. I want to be loved in order to feel lovable, but to actually take in the love of others, I have to believe I deserve it; I have to know that I am lovable already. It has taken hard work and tears and seeing myself as I really am, but now, finally, there is, deep in the very core of my being, a mother-self whose love is so profound, so unconditional, so permanent that I know that I am, forever, home. I know that she is me and I am her. This me, this I, this child and this adult, this growing, changing, struggling womanself needs and deserves an unconditional, for-all-time-and-all-places, no-questions-asked, full, deep, wet, nourishing, unafraid, and permanently committed lover—and that lover is me! And I remember, when I need to make choices and decisions about how to live and how to be, that loving myself is not an option, but a decision, a commitment that is not open for negotiation. The more I love myself, the more love flows to me from the world, and the more I have to give back. I am a *woman loving myself!*

*I*n the autumn of 1994, I sat with my spiritual director in the quiet of the monastery after evening prayer. I had not expected this visit; in fact, I was on my way out of the chapel to return to my hermitage when he intercepted me in the dim light of the gathering space. I barely saw him, so intent was I on keeping my silence, practicing custody of the eyes with my gaze cast downward and my energy contained and centered. I had already been in the hermitage and in constant prayer for seven days, my solitude punctuated only by my attendance at mass in the mornings and later, compline, prayers before bedtime, both of which happened in the chapel with the monks. Suddenly realizing that at this hour it would be strange for someone to be coming in instead of going out of the chapel, I looked up just as he spoke my name and invited me to join him for a conference. I was startled and somewhat flustered and felt completely unprepared.

I had planned on seeing him the next day and had developed a carefully considered list of questions to bring him, concerned not to waste the richness of silence or the preciousness of his gift of time on trivial chitchat or silly, petty worries. But there I was, my carefully crafted list back at the hermitage, sitting across from him in the "reconciliation room," he in a wool cap, sweater, and jeans, and I in a loose pair of sweatpants and -shirt. Not very ceremonious, this, no high ritual or drama, at least none that anyone might see. I took a deep breath and asked Spirit to guide me, to open my ears and my heart that I might hear what God has to say to me through this man, my teacher and spiritual guide. "I surrender to the unfolding mystery of my life," I reminded myself as I settled into my chair. After a few pleasantries and updates, I began our conversation in earnest.

"I don't know why to stay alive," I said, with little affect, the week of silence having quieted my emotions considerably. "It's not that I want to die, or that I'm suicidal. It's just that . . . " I paused, searching for the words that could communicate this state of being without making me sound depressed or despairing, which I was not. "I mean, it seems that I will probably be alive for a while," I continued, "but I just can't find a good reason for why, why to be alive. What am I supposed to be getting out of this? What am I missing? If the point of this life is to develop a relationship with God, to come to know God, and to love God with one's whole heart and soul and mind, it seems to me that it will be easier after life, without a body and when I'm actually with God, than it is now. I know this sounds childish, stupid even, but it's truly the question that has been absorbing me for months. What is the reason for living?"

He paused for a few minutes before breaking into his characteristic grin. He looked right into my eyes and said with perfect clarity and complete tenderness: "Well, you're not here alone, you know." He waited, and I felt the words penetrate like an arrow shot with utter precision into the depths of my being. The days of prayer had left me defenseless, wide open to each moment and to the energy of the words. The arrow found its target, exploding into knowing that spread from the epicenter like the aftershock of an earthquake rearranging form. He continued in a quiet, unhurried voice.

"After fifty years in the monastery, this is what I have learned: The only thing that really matters is love. That's all there is!" he exclaimed. "Just love. Our only job, our only work, ultimately, is to become a more and more transparent vehicle for the transmission of the divine love to each other." He paused and then began again, still more softly. "The soul whose life you are to touch may not have even been born yet." We rested in the stillness for several minutes. "That's a good reason to live, isn't it?"

I could not speak. I could only remain motionless as the energy of the words surged through me. Of course. Yes, of course. How could I have forgotten? I was thinking the words, but I could not say them. All I could manage was to thank him, softly, and we abided in the fullness of the si-

lence for a few more minutes before we each adjourned to our solitude once again. I walked the half mile back to my hermitage in the brilliance of the full moon, the words That's all there is, really, just love *soaking me from the inside out in a light and wonder and gratitude more brilliant still than the moon in all its glory.*

I Am a Woman Nurturing Myself

W hen we travel on an airplane, the flight attendant reminds us that in the event of a change in cabin pressure an oxygen mask will drop down in front of us. If we are traveling with someone who needs assistance, we are instructed, we *should put on our own mask first* and *then* assist the other person. It makes perfect sense that we cannot be of much help to anyone else if we have passed out from oxygen deprivation. And yet, as women, we so often forget this simple logic in living our daily lives. If I want to nurture other people, or projects, dreams, or visions, I have to nurture myself first. If I wait until there is no one else who needs assistance before making sure that I am getting enough oxygen, it may be too late. Because I matter and because I want to give from an abundance of inspiration, not from my last gasps, I make sure to take time to be a **woman nurturing myself.**

I Am a Woman Caring for My Friend

*S*he called me and said only one thing—"Can you take a break and meet me at Tom's?" I have to admit, I hedged. I was writing and felt that I was on a bit of a roll. But I was writing about friendship and I didn't miss the irony that I was actually thinking about saying no. "Of course, I'll meet you there in fifteen minutes," I replied. Once inside Tom's, a vintage burger bar, we ordered our ritual fare. Usually careful eaters, we go to Tom's when we need real food, comfort food, grounding food. When my friend asked me to meet her there, I knew that this was what she needed.

So we devoured burgers with the works, french fries, and the most essential ingredient of our ritual meal, onion rings. Over the feast my friend talked and cried, sharing how it is to continue to try to go on living after a husband commits suicide; talking about healing, talking about forgiving, talking about finding a new path, a new identity, a new self; losing herself, finding herself, two steps forward, one step back; one step forward, two steps back. Salt, ketchup, onion rings, steak sauce, tears, laughter, touching, hugging. Women. Friends.

When we were leaving, she hugged me and said, "Thanks for coming. I needed this, needed some soul food. Tom's and Janet, that's just what I needed, soul food." I came back to my desk feeling full—and not just from french fries and onion rings. I am a *woman caring for my friend.*

I Am a Woman Following My Heart

*B*oth my mind and my heart are my allies. I listen carefully when my mind warns me, when it helps me to identify the risks and the benefits of options I am considering. But when I am really caught between two options, I will always go with my heart, that abundant fountain of feelings and the chalice containing all that I love. It knows, as no other part of me knows, the truth of my deepest longings, the things that make me laugh and the things that reduce me to a puddle of tears. It knows what is real and what is only a mirage.

Almost every time I am caught between my mind and my heart, my mind is being run by fear, while the longing of my heart is for freedom and love. If I am going to err, I would rather create too much love than too little; be too foolish rather than too fearful. When I look in the mirror, I would rather see someone who is a little scared and a lot loving than be greeted by a grim face smug with certainty and eyes dull with carefulness. When my life is over, I want to look back and regret the mistakes I actually made, not the ones I was too afraid to make. I am a *woman following my heart.*

I Am a Woman Allowing Others to Be Right

I once attended a couple's workshop with my (then) partner. The leader had us do an exercise moving our hands and our bodies together with one person leading and the other following. I had the experience that my partner was leading. I felt that he was subtly pushing me, that he wouldn't allow me to lead him, and I thought how this was just *so* typical. When the exercise was over, we were instructed to share our experiences. I shared mine first, with not a little bit of irritation. Then, in a state of complete disbelief, I received the news that my partner had had the opposite experience. He said that he was following me, in fact was really enjoying following me, and wasn't resisting me at all.

I became really angry—not only was he resisting me as usual, but now he was lying about it in front of the whole group and making me look like a fool. I said that I knew what I saw, I knew what I felt—and he *was* resisting me. "No, I *wasn't*. I absolutely was *not* resisting you!" I was ready to throttle him.

When the workshop leader finally called time out I expected her to tell my partner that, indeed, he was wrong, and that even she could see that he *was* resisting me and that he *was* leading. Instead, she said that we had just demonstrated perfectly the point of the exercise—that two people can be engaged in the same process and have completely different experiences of it—*and that there was no right or wrong, just different experiences.* I couldn't believe it. How could I possibly *not* be right and he, *not* wrong? But she insisted that we were each right in our own experience of the event. I felt humiliated, which told me something about how attached I was to being right. My partner was thrilled because I frequently got into this kind of an argument with him—making him wrong because he was having a different experience than I.

Since then, I've gradually gotten better at being able to say: "I can't imagine how you could (fill in the blank _____ think that, do that, feel that, believe that, etc.), but I respect your right to be different from me." The hardest part has been letting go of the idea that there *has* to be a *right* and a *wrong* in any conflict. Learning that there doesn't have to be, that in fact there can be two rights, has been a great liberation for me. It allows me to relax more, even in the midst of a conflict, and really hear what the other person is saying. So when I find myself gearing up to fight for my position, I choose instead the freedom of being a woman *allowing others to be right.*

A Reflection: ON WOMAN AND WAITING

everal years ago I moved from full-time to part-time work at the university, teaching one course a year for seven percent of my annual salary. I didn't know how I was going to survive financially, but I did know one thing: I was going to have my life, my one, true, authentic life, whatever it took. My commitment to myself as a woman finding my voice is that I will no longer live in ways that aren't true for me. As I have tried to live my commitment, I have discovered that it involves more waiting than anything else.

We despise waiting in our revved-up, full-speed-ahead world. In the grocery store where I shop, there are now six self-serve checkout stands. One doesn't have to waste time while some gangly adolescent with an earring in his eyebrow leisurely saunters through the groceries looking for bar codes. Now we can whiz through it ourselves—no waiting! We won't tolerate being on hold for more than a few seconds, and waiting for the files to load on our increasingly faster computers makes us crazy. We want instant messages *over the Internet instead of messages conveyed in the sluggish old-fashioned way of sending a fax and waiting until later that day for an answer. We have call waiting on our phones, which is really not call waiting but call* not *waiting, saying* don't *keep me* waiting, take me now! *And more and more people I see every day are attached to electronic leashes because someone may need them to respond* right now. *They simply mustn't be kept waiting.*

In a world dominated by doing, achieving, producing, and getting, waiting is seen as an enemy. Yet this is only half of the story about waiting. It seems to me that there is something decidedly feminine about waiting. In day-to-day life, women are always waiting for something or someone. We wait for womanhood to announce her arrival, supplies carefully tucked away until the big day when they are required. We wait every month to be visited by our friend or the curse, depending on one's perspective and how anxious one is about its arrival. We wait in gynecolo-

gists' offices or family planning clinics at least once a year. We wait for phone calls from suitors, invitations to date, and the arrival of our suitor at the correct time. We wait for first kisses and marriage proposals. We wait for nine months for the new life within to become the new life without and we wait to go on with our lives while we tend our newborns and sore nipples, in that order. We wait until our families have enough to eat before getting our food and until our children are sleeping to get to the bathroom. We wait in the waiting rooms of pediatricians and dentists, principals and dance teachers. On and on the waiting goes. We get lots of practice in waiting, which can actually help us when all we can do is wait for the next right step to become clear.

Waiting is like the pause between breaths; it's what separates one event from the next, what has happened from what will follow. We do something, then we wait. Then we do something else, then we wait. This in-between time is not empty, but is a space for transitions, for closure and mulling over and reflecting, and for thinking ahead, deliberating, discerning. Far from wasting time, waiting, when it is done consciously and with intention, is a superbly right use of time.

Waiting is the womb preparing each month to receive new life; it is the empty clay pot full of potential; it is the deep feminine principle of receptivity and intuition, of allowing and being still. Waiting is the only way to learn about what wants to happen in us, what wants to birth itself from our depths, what we are to do with our one precious, unfolding life. Without this part of the process, the balancing in our own being of the feminine energy of waiting with the masculine energy of doing, our souls may refuse to reveal themselves. The soul speaks in quiet moments of waiting, in its own time, which, by the way, is always perfect.

I Am a Woman Bathing in the Bliss of the Company of Other Women

*S*itting in a circle, women beside me; women across from me; women around me; women embracing me; women supporting me; women listening to me; women understanding me; women appreciating me; women admiring me; women comforting me; women laughing with me; women keening with me; women celebrating with me; women outraged with me; women creating with me; women allowing me to create my own way. Women healing each other; women healing the world; women longing for peace; women uniting for justice; women choosing love and forgiveness; women visioning; women in the world; women in the home; women mothering children; women tending men; women nursing parents; women running institutions; women struggling; women overcoming; women growing; women dying. Women, huge and tiny, bold and shy, wide and full, long and athletic; wise, strong, tender, holy, compassionate, vital, brilliant, magnificent, multicolored, multitalented, multifaceted, sparkling, glimmering, light-giving gems of Creation, women! I am a *woman bathing in the bliss of the company of other women.*

I Am a Woman Trusting Myself

*A*s a woman in this culture, I have been discouraged from turning inward for answers. But sitting by the river's edge, listening to her speak to me, within me, I have come to trust my own deep womanly essence—the core of my being as woman on this earth. My own truth lives in me like a great energy source and cannot be found anywhere else. It moves within me, prompting me toward my highest good, emerging and unfolding in absolute integrity and with complete honesty. This truth runs deep and it runs full and it runs wet and it runs free. It is as unstoppable as the river and as life-giving. It is nourishment and guidance and power. It is wisdom connected to the wisdom of all women who ever were and to the Divine itself. It is the only wisdom deserving of such a radical surrender as trust. And yet, ironically, trusting myself increases my trust in others. I know now that I can access this deep truth by taking my time and listening. And so I am, in all situations, in every time and in every place, with every person and in every relationship, a *woman trusting my self.*

I Am a Woman Childless by Choice

I am a middle-aged woman who has not borne a child. I am a woman childless because I was afraid and because abortion was an option. I didn't think much about it at the time, and neither did he. Especially, neither did he. It was easy—a short drive, a few hours, and the "problem" was solved. Afterward, we went out and celebrated with pizza and beer to break my fast. He paid, and we were relieved. Especially he was relieved. We never talked about it again. Well, he never talked about it again.

I am a woman childless by choice, keening for my unborn child so many years later. My baby comes, releases, and forgives me. Receiving absolution, which I never thought I wanted or needed, from a priest truly Christ-like, I am reminded that no matter what, I am loved, was always loved, will always be loved, by the one who has known me since before I began. I am forgiven. I have forgiven myself. I am rich in blessings, grace, and love; and still, and always, I am a *woman childless by choice.*

I Am a Woman Forgiving Men

*F*or years I have secretly blamed them, ridiculed them, and judged them. Men. The enemy. The cause for all that is wrong with the world, and in particular with my world. In college I had a bumper sticker on the wall of my dorm room—*a woman without a man is like a fish without a bicycle.* That about says it all—who needs them? Not me, that's for sure. Over the years I have loved many men, yet distrust and bitterness still lurked in my unconscious. Blaming the collective oppression of women on individual men, who are unique children of Creation just as I am, was an error I would not see for many years. There have been many costs of the error, not the least of which is the failure to do my own inner work to heal old wounds. As long as I could blame patriarchy and men, I could stay angry and avoid taking responsibility for my own healing and growth.

Make no mistake. Patriarchy is still unacceptable and the oppression and abuse of women in all its forms is repulsive. These are wrongs that must continue to be named and fought. But there are men's groups, too, naming and fighting them. And there are men whose hearts break as deeply as mine when they hear on the evening news of another battered woman, another raped child.

My life's work is about healing, wholeness, and love. Where there is not forgiveness, there is no love. I am learning that if I want to truly help the world to heal, I have to learn to love the other half of its human inhabitants. I even have to learn to love the men who are perpetrators of abuse, crimes, wars, genocide. I do not have to condone the actions, but I have to find a way to love the deep soul inside of those broken human beings. Not an easy path, but a true one. I continue to struggle to be *a woman forgiving men.*

A Reflection: ON BEING A GODMOTHER

When her parents asked me to be Faith's godmother, I was thrilled and deeply moved. I was searching my mind and heart for a gift to bring to her to acknowledge our important connection when I remembered about the tradition of the birth song. In tribal cultures children are born into the singing of their individual songs by the women surrounding the births. The mother listens for the song in the wind, or from deep within herself when the child is still in her womb, and then teaches it to the others. Throughout pregnancy, the mother will sing that song to her unborn baby, and the song will accompany the child throughout life, as a connecting thread from the time before birth until life's end.

I met Faith for the first time just a week after her birth and I sang a song to her. Words and melody made up by me, simple truth, I sang Faith Marie, Faith Marie, sweet as can be, God's gift to me. I sang it softly, over and over, as I walked the floor with her when she was fussy, giving her mom a break, or with her nestled into my bosom as we all rested on the couch. I sing it to her each time I meet her again. I sang it to her on her first birthday and I sing it to her when she grabs the phone from her mom, as a way of helping her to connect with my disembodied voice.

But there's more. There is something about singing this sweet little song that opens my heart and fills me with the most delicious, tender love, something that reminds me, over and over, of the truth of our relationship, the truth of who she is to me. Faith Marie, Faith Marie, sweet as can be, God's gift to me. This simple awareness deepens my commitment to her, strengthens my desire to be a source of unconditional love and support throughout her life. It reminds me that the most appropriate response when we have been given a precious gift is gratitude and the willingness to take care of it.

On the day we christened Faith, I took a walk with her on the beautiful grounds of the church while everyone else socialized just outside the entrance. Carrying her upright so that she could look out and see the world, I sang her her song and I wondered to myself, as her new god-mother, "Oh sweet one, precious daughter of God, how do I tell you about the One who has known you and loved you since before you were born?" And then I just began whispering in her ear as I continued our stroll. "Faith Marie, you are a perfect child of God, who loves you very, very much. God loves you so much that she made these trees and this grass and those birds and the sky and the rivers and fields and the flowers and everything that we can see here just to be sure that you have a good place to grow up in. God made your mommy and daddy and all these other people who came today just to love you, just to make sure that you always have all the love you need. And, sweet Faith, there are angels all around you, watching over you day and night, so that you are always safe, always protected, and never alone. And do you know what else, Faith? God gave me to you, to be your godmother, to walk with you on your life's journey as God the Mother would walk with you. And God gave you to me because God could see that I needed to open my heart just a little bit wider and love a little bit deeper. So you and me, we're together now, Faith, walking together as you grow, and we'll keep talking about all this as we go along, okay?" I sang her song to her again, and then we returned to her party.

My goddaughter Faith is an extraordinary blessing in my life. I pray that she never forgets who she really is—a precious child of God. And I pray in deep gratitude that my heart has been given another beautiful child to love in such a special relationship. Precious Faith, perfect child of Spirit, may I walk with you in this lifetime as one who loves you as God loves you.

I Am a Woman Doing Exactly
What I Want to Do

I am a child of the sixties and a woman of the nineties. I have choices and options that women have never had before. I am free, because of the struggles and sacrifices of so many women before me, to pursue work that satisfies my deep need to be productive and to be of service in a circle wider than the intimate band of family. I thank my sisters, past and present, for their work in the world: work that has made it possible for me to vote, to be educated, to have my own home and a serious line of credit, to apply for any job I want and at least not be told "no" outright, and to go wherever I want, whenever I want to go, alone. I am a *woman doing exactly what I want to do.*

I Am a Woman Celebrating Motherhood

*K*nit together by the Creator in our mothers' wombs, perfectly and precisely female did we emerge. Awesome miracle is womanbody made for mothering; created as sanctuary for life giving, cradle for life sustaining! Tending, holding, nurturing, comforting, mother! Carrying, rocking, lifting and letting down, mother! Clapping hands and wiping tears, moving in and backing off, mother! Connection so deep and commitment so eternal, death to her before harm to the child, mother! Connection so deep and commitment so eternal, staying alive for the child, battling cancer, suffering devastating pain, mother! Heart-opening, heart's delight, heart-broken, heart-redeemed, mother! Work so important, love so longed for, a world so needy, to nurture so precious, mother! Never again diminished by this voice, never again disparaged and made less through these eyes, mother! I am a *woman celebrating motherhood!*

I Am a Woman Saying Yes to God as Mother

I took my seat on the meditation pillow and began again. I was practicing Centering Prayer, a method of meditation that comes from the ancient Christian contemplative tradition. For the past seven days I had done only this, interspersed with meals and several short walks, all in solitude. As I tried to let go of thoughts and turn my attention to my sacred word, I was flustered and disturbed by an image that I could not seem to escape. It was Christ, but not the Christ I was used to from my Catholic upbringing or even from my recent past of reconciliation with these roots. This Christ had breasts, and each time I tried to "correct" the image, replacing it with one of my own remembering, it would reinsert itself in mind. I finally gave up trying to stop it or change it and simply let it be there while I turned my attention back to the prayer. After I finished the session, I reached for pen and paper, and this is what poured through me and onto the page:

Come, rest here a while with your God who loves you.

Come, nurse at my infinite breast;
there is sweet milk enough for billions of lifetimes.

Come, lay your head in my lap,
and remember how it feels to be home.

Come, be filled with my perfect love,
and know beyond knowledge
that love is what you are.

Come, come, come now, and give yourself to love.

I am a **woman saying yes to God as Mother.**

I Am a Woman Becoming Just

I'm *just* a nurse, I'm *just* a homemaker; I'm *just* a stay-at-home mom; I'm *just* a secretary. Why do we so often describe the womanwork we do with a word that means merely, only, as if we should bow our heads in shame, lower our eyes and our voices, justify our right to take up time and space? Why do we feel the need to apologize for the roles we have chosen to fill, the work we have chosen to do, work that so often becomes visible only in its absence, work that, when it is done well, heals people, creates sacred space, nurtures life, and facilitates the work of others?

What if we considered the other meanings of the word *just,* the first meanings—fair, upright, honest, legitimate, true, righteous in the sight of God? And what if we reversed the order of the words *just* and *a,* and claimed our justness? I am *a just* nurse; I am *a just* homemaker; I am *a just* stay-at-home mom; I am *a just* secretary? What if we meant it, believed it, aspired to it, worked toward it? Instead of lowering our heads and averting our eyes, we could look in the mirror and say, with pride and dignity, I am a ***woman becoming just***.

A Reflection: ON THE GIFT OF A FRIEND WHO LISTENS

*W*hat an extraordinary gift is a friend who listens to all that wants to be spoken; listens for however long it takes to pour out all of the story, feelings, fears, what-ifs, and maybe-nots as if she has all the time in the world. Sometimes a little sharing isn't enough and leaves one frustrated, like starting to make love, becoming aroused, and then failing to consummate. The lack of emptying, of giving one's self fully, leaves one congested with the energy of the unheard story, the untold truth about one's life and who one is and what matters and where one hurts or sings or dies a little.

With each instance of incomplete sharing the congestion builds up and one also becomes increasingly less likely to try again. This is the real danger. Eventually, there is just stagnation, an emotional numbness and unconscious withdrawal from even trying to share our stories. This numbness is often interpreted as being "just fine," as in "How are you doing?" "Just fine, thank you." And after a while one really is "just fine," living inside the shell of one's own defenses and mired in the stagnant remains of emptying prevented. It is toxic, soul killing.

So this is what my friend and I provide for each other—safe, welcoming containers into which the other may pour out the contents of a life lived and where, in the complete sharing, space is created for more living. It is such a woman thing, to enter this place of loving receptivity and to allow time for the full unfolding. Deliciously, wonderfully a woman thing. I am so grateful.

I Am a Woman Making Myself Safe

*T*here's hardly ever a real live tiger outside my door, or even a real live mugger. There's usually only me and all my old scripts and fears and projections and what-if stories. The threats to my everyday safety are hardly ever real threats to my life and limb, but are usually threats to my sense of self-esteem and belonging in the world—fears of looking foolish, or being rejected, of loving and then losing love, of being vulnerable and not being met with kindness or compassion. Yet these are real threats to my self-esteem only if I allow them to be. Trying to protect myself from these dangers by being overly careful or withdrawn limits me and my spontaneity; it makes me fearful and tight instead of relaxed and open. Life becomes much less fun and much more exhausting. There is a different way. My true safety lies not in keeping myself out of danger by avoiding the risks of fully engaging in life, but by remembering that no matter what life brings me, I am strong enough, smart enough, loving enough, vital enough, interested and curious enough to handle, learn, and grow from it. And in choosing this full, conscious openness to my life, I am a *woman making myself safe!*

I Am a Woman Loving My Friends

Without my friends I would scarcely know who I am. Female friendship is most of all about sharing who we are. It seems, from the outside looking in, that men have friends whom they *do* things with, but women have friends to *be* with. It doesn't matter to me what I do with my friend, as long as I am with her. Running errands is fine, or meeting for coffee, or eating Chinese take-out on the deck, or going for a hike. It's about just being together, which we will also do at a moment's notice if we are needed. No questions asked. We are there when life calls for a breast biopsy or a colonoscopy. We are there in the hospital waiting room while a husband undergoes surgery. We are there in each other's kitchens when one is felled by illness or injury; there in each other's laundry rooms and shopping for groceries when the new baby comes home. We are on the phone at 2 A.M. when one cannot sleep; we are on a plane at 2 P.M. when one just cannot cope. We are there at the births, the celebrations, the losses, and the deaths. We are not passive observers of each other's lives; we help each other live them. Women friends. Womanfriend. I cannot imagine my life without them. I am a *woman loving my friends.*

I Am a Woman Doing What I Know

*R*ecent scientific discoveries have shown that women who have breast cancer and belong to a support group of other women with breast cancer live twice as long as women who receive only standard treatment. Science telling us that support helps us cope and actually makes us stronger. We are women. We knew that. Studies show that men who have had heart attacks and who do not have loving relationships with spouses have a four times greater chance of suffering another heart attack than men with spouses. Science tells us that love and belonging are matters of life and death. We are women. We knew that. On and on it goes, science finally catching up to the wisdom women have always shared with each other; wisdom that has nourished centuries of human beings and kept them whole. From now on, I am not apologizing for what I know as a woman or waiting for science to prove it. I will just live and love and care and nurture, because I am a *woman doing what I know.*

I Am a Woman Forgiving Myself

*E*very spiritual tradition has a teaching on forgiveness, including the Catholic one in which I was raised. When his disciples asked Jesus how many times we should forgive each other, Jesus replied, "Seventy times seven." In other words, forgive everyone, every time. I am part of everyone, yet I often neglect to apply this teaching to myself. When I see my own selfishness and self-centeredness or when my actions wound others, I am particularly harsh to myself. Sometimes in those painful moments of awareness of what I have done, I hate myself and I feel worthless, undeserving of even simple kindness, let alone true love and forgiveness. My heart turns cold against me.

As I have grown, I have come to see that keeping myself out of my own heart is abusive. As one who is loved completely and already forgiven by God, infinitely, it is pride and arrogance, not goodness, to remain harsh and judgmental to myself. It is a lack of humility to refuse a gift, not strength of character. Worse, it is also a way to keep myself above other people, to feel better than them in a way. I can justify my "high standards" and my unwillingness to forgive others because I'm not treating them any differently than I treat myself.

None of this helps me to do what I most want to do in the world, which is to be an instrument for love and peace. Kindness, love, and compassion grow from the inside out. So forgiveness must begin with me—seventy times seven times. If I can't forgive myself, I can't truly forgive anyone else. And if I can't forgive, I can't love. I continue to pray for the grace to be a *woman forgiving myself.*

A Reflection: ON BEING AN AUNT

*H*aving a niece is one of life's sweetest treats. There is a freedom to just love this child exactly as she is, without the day-to-day responsibilities for her well-being. An aunt isn't someone the child has to love, and so the relationship must be cultivated and tended over time, without any expectations for payback.

I am Tara's aunt. While Tara was growing up, I usually visited my sister, brother-in-law, and Tara once a year, at Christmas. One of my great joys during those visits was to be first up in the morning, so that it would be just Tara and me in the early hours of the day. Two gals, one very young, one not, sharing life at the kitchen table. We have years of conversations and memories of those times, which we still enjoy recalling. One of our favorites took place when Tara was just four years old.

That morning she told me a long, involved story about how she would handle the big, bad, wolf if he came into her house. "I will get him wif the broom!" she said. She ran and got the broom and showed me just how she would get rid of that wolf, swinging and banging with all her tiny might. "I will get him," she exclaimed, "I will get that bad wolf wif dis broom!" I marveled at her fearlessness at such a young age and I was delighted to affirm her strength, courage, and power even as I let the preciousness of her little self turn me into mush.

Throughout Tara's youth I cultivated our long-distance relationship by sending books, cards, and periodic care packages. I would gather up little things from my travels—peanuts from airplanes; special pencils from airport gift shops; stickers with her name on them—and send them off. I often used a green felt box, which opened on a hinge and had a pink rose on its cover. The box was the packaging for Disaronno Amaretto, a liqueur I used to drink in those days. My sister said that Tara loved getting the packages in the mail, and so I continued this practice for years.

For Tara's sixteenth birthday I wanted to create a rite of passage for her, something we don't really have in this culture. I gave her the poem that I had written for her just before her first birthday sixteen years ago, which appears at the end of this reflection. I also composed a long letter in which I welcomed her to womanhood, celebrating who she was and who she was becoming. Finally, I crafted a set of stones from clay into which I inscribed many different affirmations appropriate for this passage in her life. It was another special time for us.

While my niece often tells me how much she loves me, I never quite realized how important all those early years of caring had been until just a few months ago. I had broken my ankle and was housebound for six weeks. I did not go through the process of dependency and immobilization well, and I shared this with Tara during a phone call. I was pretty low and also worried about gaining weight since I couldn't go for my daily run. Tara is a former gymnast (years of lessons partially and happily paid for by her aunt) and personal trainer, so I knew she would understand this concern. A week later, I received a package in the mail. Inside was a box filled with some chocolate kisses, because you need to treat yourself nicely; some gourmet jelly beans, sweet but nonfat, because I know you're worried about gaining weight; and a book, The Little Engine That Could, because I know you can. All of this was packed in—can you guess? A Disaronno box. It was a metal tin, not the old-fashioned, green felt kind, which, my niece told me, she had hunted for in liquor stores near and far. To me, it could have been made out of sawdust. In this case it was truly the thought, and the shared remembrance, that counted.

An aunt can be a comforter, a snuggler, a back tickler, a sounding board, a friend, a fan, an adviser, an advocate, a role model, a mentor, and a guide. My relationship with my niece has covered all of that terrain over the years, and more, and it is still one of the great treasures of my life. Being an aunt can provide us with a wonderful opportunity to participate in and influence the lives of young people as they grow toward their full potential. This opportunity has been especially important to me as a woman with no children of my own. All of these years after I first realized it, Tara is still a precious miracle to me, and oh, so very loved. That she loves me too is pure gold, grace without measure.

FOR TARA

How is it, little one, that in the
crystal clearness of your eyes
I find myself?
How is it that with fingers
so tiny and delicate
you can pry open my soul
and make me weep?
How is it that in comforting you
I am soothed,
and when making you laugh
I can sing again?
How can you, so fragile,
vulnerable, and dependent,
make me feel so fragile,
vulnerable, and dependent?
You are, indeed,
a precious miracle,
and oh, so very loved.

JANUARY 2, 1977

I Am a Woman Accepting Change in the People I Love

I was talking to a friend, actually a former boyfriend, when I casually said something like, "Well, that's just the way you are; you always do things that way." I hadn't meant to be hurtful, yet still he was wounded. What had hurt him wasn't that I had dismissed his behavior so quickly, which, of course, I shouldn't have. "You won't let me continue to grow," he told me softly. "You see me only the way I was then. You keep me trapped in some old box and you don't see me as I am now, today. It really makes me sad." He was right.

Sometimes we keep people we love from growing, from finding their own true paths, by insisting that they be unchanging, always the same, always predictable. There is a safety of sorts in that, a kind of security. But ultimately there is a great price—it is the freedom of the other to be who they are; to find her or his own way. When the box in which we have wanted to keep someone contained, tamed, and familiar, collapses, there is a great potential released. We have a choice: We can turn toward the change, keeping our hearts open and asking with genuine interest and willingness to learn, "Who are you now? I feel scared by this change, tell me, how does it feel to be you, now, here?" Or we can turn away from this love and reject the change, choosing the secure loneliness of our own hard hearts to the vulnerability of being with someone we really don't seem to know very well anymore.

I am learning to choose the latter. It has so much more potential for love and life! When I demand that the people in my life behave in ways that I define for them, I keep them, and me, imprisoned. When I instead access my deep feminine soul, I trust that within each person there is an authentic, true self working to develop its unique gifts, talents, hopes, dreams, and purpose. From this place, I can allow people the same freedom I desire—the freedom to become who they are most deeply meant to be. When I let go, we are all more free, and whenever even one other soul becomes just a little more free, the entire universe is born anew. I am a *woman accepting change in the people I love.*

I Am a Woman Doing Whatever It Takes to Raise My Children

*S*ingle mothers are heroines of mine. Action-packed days and sleepless nights; racing to get them all out in the morning; racing to get them picked up at dusk. Making ends meet and leftovers last; supervising homework and playing Old Maid while stirring the pot and setting the table. No one to share the burden of communicating with an endless network of other adults—teachers, doctors and dentists, coaches, the PTA, and baby-sitters. Fatigue so relentless that it feels normal; dedication so complete that it doesn't matter. Single mothers are awesome, amazing, inspiring creatures, choosing every day to keep going, keep trying, keep tending, keep loving. Quitting is not an option. After all, they are mothers, each one committed to being a *woman doing whatever it takes to raise my children.*

I Am a Woman Finding Courage
with Other Women

*O*ne out of eight women will get breast cancer. Some of them will be my friends. One of them could be me. What would I do? I hope that I would do what so many incredible women are doing—remembering that courage isn't not being afraid; courage is doing what you need to do even though it terrifies you. I hope that I would have the courage to fight hard, if that was the call; the courage to say no when the treatment felt more dangerous or dehumanizing than the disease; the courage to keep living or the courage to die well. Yet one thing seems most clear. If I received that diagnosis, I would deal with it as I have dealt with every other crisis in my life. I would surround myself with womenfriends; bathe in their love; allow their tender nurturing; let them hold me; seek their guidance and wisdom; and ask them to help me to be a *woman finding courage with other women.*

I Am a Woman Who Sleeps Alone

I am a woman who sleeps alone. Turning roughly without restraint; stretching full-out with a great bellow; rolling over to one side of the bed, then back to the other. Sheets of silk or flannel, it doesn't matter; it is all pure luxury, this bed of mine. This bed that I do not share, where there are no lines drawn down the middle that might as well be made of porcupine quills; this bed, laden with an abundance of pillows and sweet-smelling sachets, which waits for me without complaint no matter when I get there; this bed where the only noises are mine and where there is no snoring to wake me once I am asleep. I go to sleep when I choose, I wake when I choose, I watch TV or eat or read in my bed all night if it suits me. Most of all, I must confess, though it is probably quite rude of me to do so, I enjoy the fact that the only scents of nature which I must endure in my bed are mine. I am a *woman who sleeps alone.*

J am reading **Wild Mind** *by Natalie Goldberg, and she just got me. She writes, "I'm lonely and I suffer." Actually, she writes, " . . . I told her my most shameful secret. I said to her, 'I'm lonely and I suffer.' There we were at the bottom of my life."*

That sentence goes right to my heart, to the place that responds with large, salty tears blinding me to the next sentence. At the speed of light it breaks me open, plunges me into my own depths to the bottom of my life. Here, in this depth, we are kin, sisters in the land of the uncoupled.

We who live here, by choice or by chance, are indistinguishable from the others by day. Even in the evening, you might not see the difference. But in the high tide of night, there it is, the final truth. We sleep alone. There is no breath beside us, no rhythm to join with as we drift together on the swells of sleep. No warmth attracts us, like a heat-seeking missile in search of a body. There is no form outlined against the moonlit wall, rising and falling, familiar mystery beside us, a silent lullaby, motionless rocking soothing us back to our slumber. There are no arms reaching out across the abyss of aloneness, pulling us back from the edge, grounding us in space and time, holding us against solid chest, strong legs, penis at our backs, sometimes thick and ready even in sleep.

When the receding tide of darkness brings rising, there is no leave-taking, no tearing away from the succor of two, no nostalgia for the sweet comfort of the shared night. There is just rising, beginning again. And we are okay. We are blessed, happy, productive, peaceful, content. It is true, by day. It is true. But the night comes, the night always comes, when again I am a **woman who sleeps alone.**

I Am a Woman Accepting Help

*T*here are others out there, sister and brother travelers on the same journey as I am; people who are doing the best that they can to become their true selves and to live caring lives. Some can walk with me while I find my way, sharing what life has taught them. Others love me and want to help. But often I close them out in my efforts to be self-sufficient, in my fear of appearing needy or dependent, or to avoid leaving myself open to the pain of being let down. Yet sometimes life doesn't ask first, it just gives you a chance to learn a new lesson.

On a snowy morning last January I was rushing out the door to teach a class. I stepped down, slipped, and fell. I knew as soon as I tried to move that I had broken my ankle. I called two different girl-friends. A Jeep Cherokee with two husbands in it arrived up my snowed-in driveway within the hour and transported me to the emergency room, where my suspicions were confirmed. The wife of one of these husbands, herself a physician, arrived in the ER in time to help me listen to the report from the doctor. My friends loaded me into their car, shopped for some groceries, took me home, settled me in, prepared food, put water at my bedside, made sure I had enough medication for the pain, and took my new puppy with them to care for.

When I hobbled into the kitchen the next morning on my crutches, my coffeemaker had a little pink Post-it on it: *All ready to use—just turn on.* It had a smiley face at the bottom. Next to it was my coffee cup, clean and ready to fill. I burst into tears, as I did often over the following days when both women and men friends brought dinner and ate with me, shopped for me, brought my puppy for visiting hours, took me to the doctor, got my mail, drove me to church, vacuumed my house. It was, at that time, more than

I could take. I was both overwhelmed by the sweetness of their generosity and humiliated to be so needy and dependent. Ever so slowly, over the course of the next four weeks, I relaxed into the reality of my present life. I began to know a deeper truth than my illusion of self-sufficiency. And while the teacher was a temporary physical dependency, the lesson was much broader.

In my heart of hearts, I need. I need to be part of a larger whole. I need human touch and voice and connection. I need other people to share the journey with, in all its pain and beauty and wonder and mystery. I cannot grow in a vacuum, alone and isolated. More important, I no longer want to. I am strong enough now, wise enough, healed enough to stop resisting help and to say simply thank you. I am a *woman accepting help*.

I Am a Woman Enjoying My Sensuality

*L*avender bubble bath; the feel of silk; snuggling in my beloved's arms; stretching my muscles; lace; freshly cut flowers; mossy rocks wet with dew; candlelight; moonlight; spring rain; salty air thick with ocean; feather on my face and all over my body; cold, melting foods on a hot, summer night; curving canyon walls worn smooth by the rivers of ancient times; vanilla-scented lotion smoothed on slowly and gently; first light; vast open spaces; touch that barely contacts my skin; puppy breath; velvet; a baby's head against my lips; mud on the bottom of the river squishing between my toes; the scent of a freshly showered man; mist on my face from a waterfall; singing streams; a breeze caressing my bare breasts; mountain wild flowers—everywhere, anywhere, there are abundant reasons to be grateful that I am in this incredibly sensual, Spirit-filled, life-giving body of a woman. My prayer of gratitude is my appreciation for the gifts of the senses. I am a *woman enjoying my sensuality.*

I Am a Woman Seeking a Third Way

*T*here is a man with whom I once fell in love at a most inopportune time. I struggled and agonized over what to do. I knew I had to make a choice. I had to stop thinking about him, forget him, and move on with my life, or I had to believe what my intuition told me—that we would be together at the right time—and then live happily in that knowing. Each decision, no matter which choice I made, would bring relief at finally resolving the agonizing dilemma. Yet neither choice was comfortable for very long because each felt premature. I was making myself crazy with the indecision and with the alternating emotions of grief and joy. Something clearly had to change.

While I was out running one day, I had a flash of inspiration. I realized that to solve my dilemma a third possibility was required; something which was not a compromise between these choices, but which actually transcended them, uniting them in something completely new. I saw that what I had to do was to shift from looking at the situation as a problem to be solved once and for all to seeing it as an ongoing opportunity to grow. The truth of my situation seemed to be that, while it was possible that this man and I would be together in the future, I could not know that, and so I had to live my own life, now, as it was, without clinging to some idealized future, but also without grieving a fantasized loss.

My own inner wisdom had offered me an invitation to stretch myself in new ways. I had to grow large enough to hold both realities simultaneously within myself in peace and in complete trust in the unfolding mystery of my life. I had to turn my focus away from the dilemma and toward myself, and do whatever I needed to do to keep growing more spacious and more loving at the same time. This, I decided, was a wonderful use of my time and energy, because no matter how the situation turned out, I would grow from it. Most important, it allowed my heart to stay open.

I found the third way I was looking for in that situation, but I also discovered a new way to approach my life. Now when I feel that familiar tension rising, because I think I am caught in a seeming dilemma, I allow myself to shift, looking anew at the situation, and I again become a *woman seeking a third way.*

I Am a Woman Celebrating the Choices
of All Women

*W*hen I was younger and more arrogant, feet firmly planted on my career ladder, I judged women who chose marriage and stay-at-home mothering. I saw these choices as a sell-out, or at the very least a refusal to take responsibility for creating a life of one's own. What I didn't do was allow those women the same freedom I demanded for myself—the freedom to choose lives that work for them. Now I see things differently and realize that the true liberation of women will come when all women have the freedom to be whoever and whatever they choose, without derision, condescension, and judgment from other women, as well as from men. Now I passionately support every woman in finding the life path that is most true for her, whatever it may be. I am a *woman celebrating the choices of all women.*

A Reflection: ON LIVING FROM THE INSIDE OUT

*F*rom the time I was old enough to figure out what the rules of life were, I tried to be good. I was a good little girl, a good Catholic, a good student, and a good friend. I became a good nurse, a good professor, a good speaker, and a good partner. My purpose in life, which I did not realize but which has run me since I was two years old, was to stay out of trouble and to do what they asked. Keep everyone happy, and you will be safe.

Then one day something unexpected happened. I had the extraordinary privilege of receiving an award that gave me a six-month sabbatical from the university. It was a leadership award, and the specific instruction that came with it was that the time was to be used for rest and renewal—the true meaning of sabbatical, which comes from sabbath. And so I began to rest and renew. At first I actually panicked because, I discovered, I had not a clue about how to live without doing, how to simply be. I was paralyzed, which turned out to be exactly what was required.

Slowly, I stopped worrying and I began to look at my life. I listened for the faint sound of my own true voice, buried far below all of my identities and roles and accomplishments, below my shoulds and my have-tos, my fears and my hopes. I sat. I watched the sunrise and learned to identify birds. I waited. I watched the grass go from summer green to fall brown. I wrote in my journal every day, and every day I listened for her, for my authentic self. Finally, slowly, I began to hear the voice of my deep womansoul crying out for a life of my own, pleading for a chance to discover my own unique song; to dance to my own choreography; to define my own purpose, direction, and vision, separate from what the world expected of me; separate from trying to be good and stay out of trouble. I heard her saying, You are enough; just you, just who you are; you are good enough. You can stop proving it now. It's safe to come out; trust me, I will lead you. Trust this process. Trust that you are not alone.

And I said yes, whatever it takes, I will do that. I may be poor, I may be alone, I may be disapproved of, I may end up living in a trailer, but I will have a life that is true for me. I will pray, I will meditate, I will rediscover my womanbody, my womenself, I will heal, I will grow, I will listen to my deep womanwisdom. I will wait until I can hear her and I will consider each thing I am asked to do with the same question: Is this mine to do? Am I called to this, now? Ever? *When the answer comes from within, not from fear or guilt, but from wisdom and with love as my highest purpose, I will say yes or I will say no.*

I have said no a lot. I teach only one course per year for the university now. I start every day by lighting a candle and sitting quietly as the rising sun floods my living room with pink, then gold. Around the candle on the table before me are many special objects, most of which have been given to me—a thank-you card, a tiny crystal, a pewter heart, a string of beads, a kaleidoscope—so many treasures, each reminding me that I am loved, that I am part of a greater whole, that life is rich in blessings and miracles and is very, very good. I meditate. I run. I write. I give speeches, workshops, and retreats. Mostly, I wait. I listen. I watch. I live. I am ecstatic!

I Am a Woman Sharing Stories

Women's lives are meant to be shared with each other. I am certain of this because it is what we inevitably do. Leave almost any two women alone together and soon the revelations begin. When my friends and I get together, it is to get caught up on the unfolding stories of our lives. We encourage each other, cheer each other on, boost each other up, hold each other when we take a fall. We laugh, we cry, we cheer, we boo, we respond. Mostly that's it—we respond to each other's stories as if they are the most important stories we have ever heard. And they are. They are the stories of our friends, and it is our privilege to hear them. To be trusted with the deep truth of any other human being is an extraordinary gift. To be given the chance to listen, respond, and share our own stories in return—this I call womanheaven! One of the great pleasures of my life is to be a *woman sharing stories.*

I Am a Woman Longing for Her

*T*here is something inside me aching for expression and freedom, a restlessness that tells me I am not yet grown or complete. I know this unfolding, this becoming is in me as the tree is the acorn. It isn't narcissistic or self-absorbed to wonder about the possibilities, about the fulfillment of my purpose, my path. It is not a waste of time or money when I invest in pursuing *her,* the fullness of who I am. She is my destiny, and it is my birthright to become *her*. This urge toward becoming is the most natural thing in all of Creation, hardwired into our cells. When I honor my longing, when I support it and nurture it and give it what it asks, I affirm without apology or fear that I am a ***woman longing for* her**.

I Am a Woman Taking Time for Myself

*H*ow often have I heard myself and other women say, "When I find the time I'm going to _____" Fill in the blank: go to the gym, soak in a hot bubble bath, meditate, go to lunch with my friends, read that book I've been wanting to get to, take a few days off. We prioritize our days based on doing the things that seem to have the greatest consequence if they don't happen—such as getting the overdue report done, or the groceries bought, or paying the bills before they turn off the utilities. But in the long run, there are far greater consequences to consistently denying ourselves needed time for our own rest, renewal, and healing. There is never any spare time to be found for things we have put on the bottom of our to-do lists, which is usually where we have put taking care of ourselves. We need to move ourselves up on the list and not wait until we can find the time to care for ourselves. We have to *take* the time. After all, there are a lot of people counting on us—we need to keep ourselves whole and happy. And besides, we deserve it. I am a *woman taking time for myself.*

I Am a Woman Surrendering to the Unfolding Mystery of My Life

*N*o matter how much I wish otherwise, I can't predict what happens next in the unfolding mystery of my life. This lack of control sometimes feels frightening, yet there is an amazing freedom in it that brings a deep curiosity and sense of wonder. The most awesome and delicious experiences I have had have almost always been those that, in a million years, I could never have foreseen. I still have my hopes and preferences and I work to achieve them. Yet when I insist on some fixed idea of how my life *should* look, what I *should* be doing, how I *should* be feeling, I seem to create resistance to the natural flow. When I remember that I am part of a vital, creative process that is so much larger than my own individual self and that I am not alone in this process, that I am held always in the loving embrace of the Divine, I relax. I let go and I become a ***woman surrendering to the unfolding mystery of my life.***

A Reflection: ON BECOMING A CHAMPION OF TOUCH

*T*ouch is sometimes abused. Some people use touch inappropriately to molest children, and this terrifies us all. Some teachers have molested young students. Some priests molest grade-school parishioners. It must stop. Of this there can be no doubt. But how?

Some communities are passing new laws designed to protect the children. Attorneys are meeting with schoolteachers to educate them in the new standard of acceptable behavior. It turns out that one proposed solution to the problem of abusive touch is to focus not on the offenders but on touch itself. The approach to the problem doesn't ask how can we get a better handle on these disturbed people or how can we raise people who know how to use touch appropriately. No. The solution to the problem of people who abuse touching is to stop all people from touching.

So now schoolteachers are told that if they are caught touching a child, they could lose their jobs. And what message is given to the child who runs to his teacher crying and is repelled? How does this boy learn about good, safe, nourishing touch, about getting support when he feels hurt or sad? Where does he get enough good touch so as not to grow up to seek touch in abusive ways?

Psychotherapists are afraid to offer a hug to a crying client, or even to put an arm around a shoulder when the client is leaving. Psychotherapy has become a strictly no-touch practice. Yet the withholding of appropriate human touch is at least as immoral as the crimes we are trying to prevent. Suffering human beings are denied the benefit of what is one of the most powerful healing tools we have—our caring and compassionate touch. If this is not immoral, what is?

The most ludicrous example of just how crazy this is getting comes from a recent conversation I had with a young psychiatrist. He has just completed studies in energy medicine and massage therapy. I asked him why he did that. Did he intend to leave medicine to do massage? "No," he said. "But I want to be able to touch people and to do healing work with them. Now I have a license that allows me to do that." A physician training in energy medicine and massage so he can actually practice healing and legally touch patients—how far will this madness go? What are we thinking?

If anything is clear it is that we are a society in need of more, not less, touching; more, not less, nurturing; more, not less, caring. We need to be touched. Touch conveys something essential to the entire body-mind-spirit. It tells us that we matter. It tells us that we exist, that we belong, that we are not isolated strangers floating alone through time and space. Touch grounds us in the here and now, bonds us to incarnation, tells us that embodiment is a gift, pleasurable, safe. Touch tells us that we are good, welcomed, deserving of time and attention. Touch lets us know that we are still alive, still here, that we haven't slipped into some dimension between life and death. Touch comforts us, soothes us, nourishes us—literally. When we are touched, the skin releases a rush of chemicals that are good for both the toucher and the touched.

Touch is the first language of woman because it is the language of connection and relatedness. It is the language of the body, the instinctual self. Not even animals need to be told to pick up their babies, to hold them and soothe them and rock them. As women, we must, we absolutely must, speak for touch in every forum we can. To allow our society to slip any farther into this isolating, touchless, fear-based mentality can only be disastrous in the long run. Please, become a woman who is a champion of touch.

I Am a Woman Trusting My Intuition

*S*ometimes I become irrational. Sometimes I am operating out of some other center than my rational, thinking, analytical mind. Sometimes I am following the promptings of another center; something closer to the heart, or the gut; something primitive, old, instinctual; something that wells up from the depths of my knowing or pours down from the height of my connection to Source, to the ancient ones, to truth, to the entire universe of possibilities. Sometimes I just have a feeling; other times, an image comes, or a sentence in a book hits me when I've been pondering some decision. Whatever the source, I have learned to pay very close attention. To ignore these promptings is usually not in my best interests. This irrationality, sometimes called women's intuition, is often demeaned and dismissed as an invalid way of knowing. After all, where are the objective data? One cannot trust something as irrational as intuition, can one? I can. I do. I am a *woman trusting my intuition.*

I Am a Woman Becoming Fearless

*S*everal years ago, the work with which my career has been most closely associated came under rigorous attack by a group of self-described skeptics. They used the media well and often. They went to the state legislature and they petitioned the university, including the board of regents, the chancellor, and the president, to get this content out of our school. With each new round of attack, there was a media frenzy, and I became more frightened. As the hoopla died down and I calmed down, I thought I would recover. But I never did quite recover, and slowly, over several years of this battle, I became exhausted, depressed, and withdrawn. It was at this time that I received an award that allowed me to have a six-month sabbatical from the university.

With time to reflect, I came to realize that my fear was a fear of being humiliated and ridiculed. Deeper than that there was a fear that this work I had loved, to which I had given nearly twenty years of my life, would not survive. And deeper still I feared that if the work didn't survive, it meant that I, in some way, would not survive. If my work was discredited, if I actually lost my job, who would I be? I had to remember my deepest knowing.

I am a child of the Divine. I am held in the sure and steady hand of unconditional love and mercy. My life is guided, and forces beyond my wildest imaginings conspire to bring me exactly what I need. When I remembered that, when I remembered that I am not my work, my job, my titles, my achievements, then I became unafraid of losing any of them. This is called freedom, and free is a very powerful way to live. It is the gift that was hidden in the torment of those years.

In a difficult situation, I don't always recognize the gift when it is first delivered, but I am learning that in time, if I pay attention, I will see its perfection. I have come to know, through experience and not belief, that my ultimate good matters and is being brought to fruition through all the events of my life. I reject teachings that my suffering is given so that I can learn and grow, yet I trust that the creative energy of life itself will use everything that happens to bring me closer and closer to the fullness of who I am becoming. Confident in this, I am a *woman becoming fearless.*

I Am a Woman Being Patient with Myself

When I see where I want to be, who I want to be, how I want to be, and where I am now, I often become impatient with myself. I want to fast-forward and reach my goal *today*. I want to be kinder, more loving, less critical *today*. I want to be better organized and more productive *today*. The constant appraisal of my progress inevitably leads to frustration and makes me irritable, which only reinforces my sense of failure and does nothing for my ability to achieve my goals. For example, I find myself more irritable with everyone else that day, like with the slow driver in front of me, who, I discover as I scowl to my right while passing, is an elderly woman doing the best she can and who is my future, if I am lucky, looking back at me. I feel awful, and on it goes.

When I can let go and trust that my growth is guided and the timing of change is always perfect, I become much more relaxed. And, when I am more relaxed, I am generally much kinder, more loving, less critical, better organized, and more productive. So I realize that the best way for me to stay on the path of my own growth and wholeness is to state my intentions clearly and then to be a *woman being patient with myself.*

I Am a Woman Discovering
My Hidden Strength

*N*one of us gets through life without pain and suffering. Yet for some reason we often interpret our times of suffering as signs of something wrong or bad in our lives. When I remember that life simply is, that all of us will someday lose something that is precious, someone who is precious, I see suffering as a natural part of my life, as natural as my joy and pleasure. It isn't wrong, or bad. It's life lived in touch with the truth.

And I notice something else. Without fail, when life asks of me painful things, I find within me resources I didn't know I had, like resilience and a fierceness of spirit, a willingness to try again, to go on, to struggle. I have discovered, too, quieter strengths; the strengths of the feminine. I have become someone who can wait for the right time to act, the right thing to say, the right moment to offer a tender touch. Suffering has helped me find the strength to let life have all of me, to let my heart be broken open by the tragedy of another or by my own loss.

Perhaps most important, I have found that, in spite of suffering, or maybe even because of it, I still choose to say yes to life. This knowing has given me the confidence and the courage to face future difficulties as a *woman discovering my hidden strength.*

A Reflection: ON LEARNING ABOUT GRIEF

J was a nurse's aide, barely seventeen years old, when the young woman was admitted to my assigned room. She was very sick, but the doctors could not determine what was wrong with her. Within a very short time of her admission a full-scale resuscitation effort was required and failed. During the chaos, I had stood removed from the bedside and out of the way. I saw the woman's husband appear, a terror in his eyes that I, so young, had never seen before. "We've got two children," he howled as a nurse led him away from the door.

When he was allowed to return to visit the lifeless body of his wife, he could only stand there, shaking his head back and forth, very slowly, back and forth, side to side as tears dropped one by one on the white sheets beneath his hand. When he left to attend to his children, I was alone to prepare the body for the morgue. I couldn't grasp the reality of what had happened. Even though I was there for the entire event, I could not believe that it had happened, that it was real.

Before I began any of the other care, I took a large cotton pad in my hand. I stared at the face of this woman, who the doctors said was dead, who I knew was dead, but I couldn't take it in. I brought the pad slowly down toward her face. I waited. Surely she would object. Nothing. I let it drop onto the skin. Now, most certainly she would react. Still nothing. Finally, in a move so utterly raw that it is etched in my memory forever, I applied a gentle pressure to the pad, squeezing her cheeks and her nose. Still, nothing, damn it, no response. Ever so slowly, my mind began to understand. It is real. She is dead. Now you see it; now you don't. Then you were here; now you are not. I slowly proceeded with my care of her body, grieving for her husband and her children as I washed her, ticketed her big toe, and wrapped her. "This is how it ends," I thought. "This is where it's all headed." I prayed for the family on the following Christmas, their first without her. I was learning about grief.

Throughout my career as a nurse I have had many occasions to learn more about grief. Yet my deepest teaching, at least up until now, was when I was not a nurse losing a patient but a daughter losing a mother. I wrote a poem about it one evening after returning from the hospital where my mother was being treated.

Sitting there, talking, laughing, sharing,
    as we have done for years,
        it is easy to forget.
It is easy to feel that things are all as they should be;
    the same as ever;
        the same as yesterday was;
            the same as tomorrow will be.
But the nurse interrupts my fantasy
    with your afternoon medication,
        and I remember.
And I wish that there would be no more tomorrows;
    that time would stand still;
        that it would always be today.
Because I know that too soon
    there will be a very different tomorrow;
        a tomorrow without you,
            all tomorrows without you.
And for the first time, I understand the meaning of grief
    with my soul instead of my mind.

When I brought my mother home from the hospital, there were good days and bad days, and this is how it goes with people who are dying. One afternoon she dozed on the couch as I sat nearby. A sudden wave of anticipatory grief completely overtook me. This poem describes it.

I sit watching you sleep,
   your breathing easy and even,
      the lines of worry and fear
         temporarily erased from your face,
            the gentleness of your smile
               present even now.
You look so peaceful,
   but it is too much.

   I am overwhelmed with the pain
      and the emptiness of what is to come.
         I wonder, again, how long
            there's no way to tell
               really is,
   and I weep,
      knowing it could never
         be long enough.

Grief, our longing for that which we have lost, can rip us open heart and soul and leave us exhausted and gasping for air. Yet it is for precisely this reason that I see grief as a friend. Grief is a measure of our humanity. It is the currency of our belonging, the price we pay without reserve; it is our gift to those we have loved that we willingly suffer their loss. Grief is one of the consequences of a life in which one chooses to care and it reminds us, perhaps more clearly than any other experience, that we are not here alone. Finally, there is no better teacher than grief to deepen our appreciation of the present. Grief teaches us to celebrate the ordinary, simple things in our lives while we have them, because everything, and everyone, will one day pass out of this world and into the next.

Today she made me pancakes.
  She hasn't felt well enough
    in these past months
      to walk very far,
      or sit for very long,
      or read a book,
      or laugh at a joke,
      or really enjoy
      a good cup of coffee
      and a nice long chat.

But today *she made me pancakes.*
  They were the best pancakes
    I ever ate.

I Am a Woman Nurturing the Man I Love

*W*hat could await me in life more precious than this? Here you lie in my arms under azure sky serenaded by the river, and nothing else matters. No space, no time, just here, just now. I drizzle gentle fingers across your face, tracing lines, following forms, drinking you in, memorizing every mark. Sweet face, your face. You, heavy-hearted and exhausted, slip into sleep; I inhale your breath. You stir, then awaken wide-eyed and apologetic for leaving. I cuddle you closer, reassuring you that all is well. I kiss your forehead and nuzzle your cheek. Sleep returns and gratitude sweeps through me like the flowing waters of the river. That I have been given just this one, this sweet, gentle, bold, courageous one to love, to hold, to comfort, to soothe, to cradle with tender care and affection—what abundant blessing has anointed me! How I must be loved by Spirit to have been given you. I am a *woman nurturing the man I love*.

I Am a Woman Being Gentle with Myself

*T*here is so much more that I want to do in this life, so much I want to become. Sometimes it seems that the more I grow, the more clearly I see how far I have to go, and I can become harsh with myself, impatient, critical, and even hateful. Yet these reactions to my imperfection don't help me grow. They just show me why seeing myself clearly isn't a good idea, and my growth slows down. If I want my deep self to keep unfolding and becoming, I must make for it a safe place into which it can be born. When I can see my brokenness with the eyes of compassion instead of judgment, I heal and I become more compassionate with the brokenness of others. Healing always happens when I choose to remember to be a *woman being gentle with myself.*

I Am a Woman Opening to Guidance

*G*od, Holy Spirit, divine love and light is available to me, ready to help me discern which path to choose, with which timing, with which people, for which purpose. All that is required of me is that I be willing to listen and to learn to let go of my attachments to particular outcomes. This is a lifelong learning project, and so, day by day, I practice. I sit by the river and I ask: "Sister river, sister river, what have you to show me today? Sister river, sister river, what have you to teach me today?" I listen. I take my time. I write down what Spirit shares with me through the song of the river's flowing waters.

Or I light a candle at my little table in the living room and use my breath to quiet me down, focusing on the gentle rhythm, in and out, in and out. I allow a question to emerge in my mind and I ask Spirit for an answer that might help. I write down whatever comes to me, even if it isn't to my liking or doesn't make sense. I write it down even when I suspect that I'm just making it up. I don't act on everything I receive. But I always write it down. It is my way of communicating that I am serious about this and also that I am willing to let go of my ideas of what the answer *should* be.

I am a slow learner. Spirit loves me anyway and continues to speak to me through all the events of my daily life. More and more, I am a *woman opening to guidance.*

I Am a Woman Choosing to Care

*C*aring has become increasingly suspect in our modern culture of looking out for number one. When we show our concern or offer help to another, we are at risk for being labeled "codependent," a word I have come to abhor, even by the one to whom we are reaching out. Women, in particular, are lectured for caring too much, and caring itself, because it has for so long been associated with women's nurturing and tending roles, has come to be seen as weak, unwise, and even foolish.

To care for something is to really see it; to pay attention with a willingness to be called out of ourselves in response. If it is a cherished musical instrument, we will attend to its cleaning and polishing and tuning. If it is a plant, we will notice when it needs water, fertilizer, or a new pot. Sometimes I actually think I can hear my thirsty plants calling to me, though there is not a sound in the room. Caring, especially caring for people, is most of all a state of mind and heart that is attentive and open to relationship, even if that opening is for a moment, passing another person on the street and smiling instead of ignoring them. And herein lies the great adventure and challenge of caring.

Caring is not weak, foolish, or codependent but the strongest, most courageous act we are capable of, because it makes us vulnerable to each other, open to hurt, disappointment, struggle, and heartache. And it might take time, of which we have grown more possessive than we might be of gold. Caring means we don't just walk away when the going gets tough; instead we search heart and soul to find the strength to keep involved, keep trying, keep loving. Caring is fulfilling the deep call of our womanhearts for connection, belonging, and relationship. And because these are the deepest callings of our hearts, not to care is to betray our very selves. Not to care because we are afraid of the consequences is to withdraw from life itself. It is to say no to the flow of energy through us that connects us to all of Creation. It is to deny our hearts their deepest source of satisfaction and pleasure.

As women, we are well aware of the dangers of caring too much for others without caring for ourselves. But these are not two ends of a continuum, two choices between which we must decide—I care *either* for myself *or* I care for others. I care for myself *in* my caring relationships with others. I care for others by making sure that my caring comes from a place of health and fullness within me. I know I cannot solve everyone's problems, or anyone's problems, really. But I can see each one I meet as a precious human being. I can say, with heart open and eyes full of love, that you matter. In this moment, love dances between us. I am a ***woman choosing to care.***

A Reflection: ON HER DAUGHTER, THE NURSE

*J*t had been a good ballet class, fun and energizing. The class had been a gift from my mother, to get me out of the house, and I took her up on it. I had been spending most of every day sitting with her, cooking, paying the bills, or taking calls from her friends at work, everyone enthusiastically noting how much they were looking forward to her returning, yet knowing in their hearts that the day would never come.

Returning home, I walked out to the patio where I had left her to enjoy the sunshine, and I knew something was wrong. She turned her head toward me, eyes full of shame and despair, face ashen, lip quivering. "Mom, Mom," I said gently as I moved closer. "What is it, what's wrong?" And then I knew. I saw the reddish-brown dampness coming through her robe over the area of her colostomy, and my nose confirmed what I began to realize had happened. Her bowels, which had been sluggish for several days, had suddenly emptied. She was covered in the overflow of the broken seal, unable to help herself, unable to stand or walk for fear of making the mess worse. So she was forced to wait. Wait, sitting in her own feces, the smell wafting all around her, for her girl-child, her firstborn, her pride and joy, her daughter, the nurse, to return and clean up her shit.

In that moment, she wanted to die. In that moment, I would have died for her. I would have done anything to spare her. The best I could do was to set about the cleanup with calm competence, as I had done so many times in my nursing career, assuring her all the while that it was all right, that it was my fault for not making sure that this didn't happen. We never talked about it again, but something changed that day. Pride completely shattered and fear of a repeat performance always there, she seldom emerged from the bed. Even as I write twenty years later, I could weep. Cancer is brutal.

The truth of my life as woman is a truth composed of every variety of experience—glorious and mundane; heart opening and heart breaking; brutal and redemptive. It takes all of it, all of the experience, to compose the voice that speaks now. And while there were moments of horror in caring for my dying mother, there were also moments that can only be described as transcendent and sacred.

Perhaps most dramatic of these was the enormous sense I had at the instant of my mother's death at home, surrounded by her children, that in caring for her until she died, I had fulfilled some deep and singular purpose for being. I wrote in my journal several months later that "anything else I accomplish with my life will be icing on the cake. My existence has mattered."

In my dark moments, when I am hungering to know why I am here, what I was born for, what I am supposed to be doing, I remember that, and I relax, giving myself over to the bliss of living, rather than the struggle of trying so hard to do it right. I am still, gratefully, her daughter, the nurse.

I Am a Woman Owning My Fears

I am a woman becoming fearless, but I'm not there yet. Sometimes, when I am afraid, I want to deny my fear, because it feels like a step backwards. I want to keep moving, keep growing more and more courageous. Then I remember that courage isn't being without fear, it's not letting fear stop me. So true courage requires not that I deny my fear, but that I own it, name it, see it for what it is, and listen to its concerns. If I deny the fear, try to ignore it or bury it, I can't move through it, and so courage never gets to emerge.

Sometimes life is really scary, and denying that I am afraid because I am trying to live up to some image of myself is not kind or compassionate; it is harsh, unrealistic, and undeserved. My power comes not from denying my fear, or any other part of me, but from knowing more and more of the truth of who I am, including what scares me. The more I own of my true self, the more choices I have, and the freer I get. I am a *woman owning my fears.*

I Am a Woman Becoming More Self-aware

*S*elf-awareness is my ally. What I cannot see in myself I cannot claim—to celebrate or to heal. When I allow myself to see myself clearly, to see my strengths and beauty as well as my brokenness, my shortcomings, and even the things that feel too awful to see, I become more and more free. The parts of myself that I don't like don't get control of me if I become aware of them. They don't run my life through old programs and habitual ways of responding to events, and so I have more options, more choices about how I want to be and what I want to do in any given situation.

Rather than looking for someone else to blame for a foul mood, for example, I begin by noticing it, naming it, and asking myself how I might be creating this mood through my own thoughts, words, or actions. Sometimes that's all it takes to change the mood. If not, I try at least to be truthful, to claim the mood as mine, rather than as something caused by someone else, and then I try to be compassionate to myself and to other people until I can change it.

This is hard work, seeing oneself clearly, but it is worth it. And it helps immeasurably in keeping relationships free from unnecessary conflict. I am committed to doing whatever I need to do to become my full womanself, fully me and fully free. I am a *woman becoming more self-aware.*

I Am a Woman Listening for My Own Voice

*S*o many voices in my head! Old voices from childhood, schools, churches. New voices from television, radio, books, newspapers, and magazines. Familiar voices of partner, friends, children, parents, bosses. Strange voices of counselors, experts, consultants, and committees. Politically correct voices. Intimidating voices. Condescending voices and cajoling voices. Enough! To live a life that is truly mine I have to be able to hear my own voice, the voice I have worked so hard to find. I take time every day, even if it's only a few minutes, to let go of all the other voices and sit in the stillness. I invite my deep truth to speak to me, and I wait, a *woman listening for my own voice.*

I Am a Woman Noticing
the Abundance of Life

*R*acing through my days barely seeing the world around me does not make me more efficient. It makes me grumpy, edgy, and impatient. When I allow myself to remain in my body (instead of trapped in my mind), receiving the input of all my senses, my whole energy shifts. I notice a tiny green shoot poking through the sidewalk and I am reminded that life is relentless. I see the magnificent display of fresh fruits and wildly colored flowers at the produce stand and I remember that life is abundant. I experience a gentle breeze that carries in it a subtle scent of honeysuckle and I know that life is sweet. Locked inside my ruminating, planning, worrying, daydreaming mind, I miss all of that. I move from place to place driven, rushed, machinelike, out of touch with myself and with the good things of life. I exhaust myself in doing. To stay open and energized as I move through my day, I remind myself to slow down just a little and to be a *woman noticing the abundance of life.*

A Reflection: ON CLAIMING MY MOTHERHOOD

*A*s I walked past the bulkhead on my way to my seat a few rows back, I heard him. A little boy, no older than seven, it seemed, was sitting in the window seat crying. He was alone in the row, waiting for the return of his parent, I assumed. But as the airplane doors were secured and final preparations were being made, he remained alone, crying. The flight attendant seemed relieved when I motioned to her that I was changing seats to sit beside the boy. At first I sat quietly, allowing him to adjust to the presence of another person in the space, though I wanted to instantly scoop him up and hold him close.

He cuddled a stuffed animal, a bunny, I think, and continued to stare out the window and cry. I finally spoke, and the boy's story tumbled out as the plane began to roll along the tarmac. He was going back to his father's house, where he lives because they are all "dee-vorced." He doesn't want to live there, but has to live there because he can't live with his mom, because she doesn't want him to live there, because she has too many problems. But he just wants to stay there, with her, for always. He was crying hard by then, and I asked him if it would be okay if I put my arm around him. I did, just as the plane revved up for takeoff. As the plane sped down the runway he pressed his face against the window and clung to the armrest. He cried harder as the plane rolled faster, and in a heart-wrenching, anguished scream I will never forget, wailed, "Moooooooommm," as the plane lifted off. My heart broke, and in that moment I would have done anything for him.

Inconsolable, he cried as I held him for many minutes of our journey. Slowly, slowly, he quieted in my arms, and when the flight attendant brought a children's pack of goodies, he was ready to look at them and explore. I answered no when the flight attendant asked, "Do you have children of your own?" But as the trip continued, I changed my answer, at least to myself. I let myself mother this one beside me and claim a part of myself, the mother, as real and authentic and true.

I am mother when I allow my heart to be broken by televised images of the children of Romania, or the Bronx, who are growing up abandoned or abused or motherless for so many tragic reasons. I am mother when I worry about what will happen to the child who goes to her teacher in tears and who doesn't get a hug because the teacher has been told not to touch the children for fear of lawsuits. I am mother when I long to adopt all the girl-children in China and give them love and support to grow up strong and proud to be women. It is the mother who lights up with joy when seeing a child smile with pride or the sheer pleasure of achieving. It is the mother who weeps for a child who drops her head or turns away in shame under the scornful glare of an adult who has forgotten that parenting is a sacred trust.

I do not have to give birth to a child to be a mother. There are children everywhere waiting for love and tenderness and nurturing. I am open to mothering them wherever I find them, with my touch, with my mind, with my heart, with my spirit, with my voice, with my vote, with my dollars. I am a **woman claiming my motherhood**.

I Am a Woman
Imagining a New Self

*M*y identity comes from many people. Parents, siblings, partners, friends, coworkers, audiences, priests; they each have some idea of who I am, and I have allowed those ideas to form *my* idea of who I am. I have been defined by the roles I fill: daughter, sister, lover, nurse, speaker, teacher, friend—on and on they go. But who am I? Underneath or beyond all these imposed identities is a real me, an authentic self, a true self, and it is at least possible that she looks nothing like any of these roles. How am I to know if I don't give myself permission to look? How can I be sure that these roles are big enough to allow all of who I am to emerge? What might I become if I allowed myself to step out of the box of other people's expectations of me? Who might I find in such freedom?

I have begun the journey it will take to live into the answers to these questions. I've let go of some major identities over the last several years, but I'm still having a hard time naming a new identity. I tell people I've been deconstructing my life one brick at a time. I still cringe when someone who knows me as a productive academic asks me what I'm doing these days, meaning what's my latest research project or academic paper.

An acquaintance who knew me in my former life asked me that question last week on the phone. In my anxiety and uncertainty about how to respond, I completely forgot to say that I am in the middle of writing a book! I don't have writer woven into the fabric of my self-identity yet. But I can imagine it, and this is where I have to start. Then I act. I write. I try on the feel of writer. I like it. A lot. If I keep writing and keep liking it, it may become a new role I freely choose. Maybe not. I don't know, as usual these days. It takes time and a certain tolerance for feeling as if one has lost one's way to redefine oneself. But one thing, thankfully, is clear: I'll never know the answers to my questions if I don't allow myself to be a *woman imagining a new self.*

I Am a Woman Full of Contradictions

I have a friend who, I always say, is the kindest person I know. She always corrects me with the words, "except with my children." I recognize her hesitance to accept my sweet praise; I, too, see my failings with much more clarity than I see my own beauty. But none of us is only one thing, only one way. Each of us, as human beings on a journey to becoming our best selves, is many different selves, and some of these selves are contradictory. I am tender and kind and forgiving; I am harsh and critical and begrudging. I am as generous as anyone I have ever met; I am so withholding sometimes that I feel like Scrooge. I am loving and gentle; I am inconsiderate and wound people with the sharpness of my words. I am completely at peace with who I am; I hate myself and feel hopeless about ever becoming a truly loving person. All of these voices belong to me. To deny any one of them for the sake of preserving some perfect image of myself is to prevent myself from ever becoming whole. I don't have to express all of these voices out in the world. But I do need to own them in the sanctuary of my own heart. I choose to accept all of these parts of me, embracing all of who I am. I am a human being; I am a *woman full of contradictions.*

I Am a Woman Choosing to
See Things Differently

One day a student revealed to our healing class that she had been embezzled out of all her money by her accountant, a trusted friend. The student is disabled. The money was given to her by her father some years ago to invest so that she would have the basics for living. Her fellow students were aghast and asked what she was going to do. She answered that, while everyone thought she should sue, she had decided not to, because it wasn't the loving thing to do. She described turning toward what had happened with a sense of openness and curiosity. "Well, here's a new experience. I've never been here before," she said she thought to herself, "I wonder what this is going to be like." Some weeks later, she discovered herself feeling freer, lighter, more peaceful than she ever had, and more her own person. "That money was hush money from my dad; an attempt to buy me off after abusing me for most of my childhood," she said. "Now I am free of it and so, of him. Now, somehow, I will find a path that's one hundred percent mine. That woman stole my money, and I could have let that destroy me. I am making a different choice. I am using her action to take back my life." We were all stunned, and I am inspired to be *a woman choosing to see things differently.*

I Am a Woman Praying the Prayer of Parenting

*O*ne of the great joys of my life is leading spiritual retreats for women. These retreats create a time away from the unending demands of modern life; a time for women to sit in a sacred circle and be still and quiet; a time for silent prayer, meditation, and simple rest. During these retreats I often hear busy mothers lamenting that they long for a more spiritual life but they cannot seem to find it. They feel like slackers, guilty that perhaps they are not disciplined enough in the pursuit of their spiritual growth. I am always astonished by this, feeling as I do that the raising of healthy, loving children is holy work; that the care of these innocents is a sacred trust; that parenting well is the deepest act of gratitude one can offer to the Creator who graced our lives with the gift of our children. So I remind these beautiful women, these caring, loving mothers, that their parenting *is* their prayer, and it is deep, and it is sacred, and it is good, and it is enough. I ask each one to remind herself, when she is finding mothering difficult, or when she is feeling guilty about not taking structured time to pray or to meditate, that I am a ***woman praying the prayer of parenting.***

A s women, we are frequently the ones to whom the caregiving responsibilities fall when our family members need help. When my mother, separated from my father, became terminally ill, I moved from New York to
California to care for her until her death. I left everything in my life, including boyfriend, job, school, an apartment, and most of its furnishings to
move there as quickly as possible. There is no doubt that it was taxing, de-
manding, even exhausting. Yet this is not the whole story. There was not only
cost, but benefit; not just the sacrifice of myself, but the opportunity to learn
more about who I was and what really mattered to me. It was an experience
of living up to my very highest potential, of giving myself without reserva-
tion in love and compassion. I learned that this is enough, especially in caring for someone who is dying. If this were all I learned, the gift would have
been well worth the price I paid. But there was more.

When I was caring for my mother, all kinds of experiences happened
to us which changed the way I think about reality forever. For example,
one day I was sitting at my mother's bedside, where I had taken up semi-
permanent residence. She was sleeping quietly, as she had been for many
hours. Perhaps out of boredom, or maybe curiosity, I decided to do Therapeutic Touch for her, but without using my hands. Therapeutic Touch doesn't
require that one actually touch the skin of the recipient, and I had always wondered if one had to use the hands at all, or if it could be done
with only the healing intention of the mind. I decided to experiment. Re-
maining motionless, I began by quieting my mind and centering myself.
When I felt calm and relaxed, I allowed feelings of comfort and love to
radiate out toward my mother. I visualized a cobalt blue cocoon of healing energy being woven around her and holding her gently. In this cocoon, all fear and pain were gone and only peace remained.

Settling into the image, I lost track of time. In what seemed a very
few minutes, my mother suddenly awoke. Turning her head toward me, she

looked soft, relaxed. So often when she woke up it was with a start, and as she looked for me she seemed fearful, panicked almost, until her eyes brought my presence to her. But at that moment, it was different. She looked at me sweetly for a brief moment and then, with a small, soft smile, said simply, "You make it so much easier." With that, she turned away and slipped easily back into sleep.

How was it possible? I was astounded. Was this just a coincidence? How did she know? I sat in wonder and awe and with questions as the events replayed themselves in my mind. I tried to figure out if there were some external cues to which she was responding, but I came up empty. And then my mind drifted to other events, other instances when there was communication between us that was beyond words, even beyond space and time, as in the following dream.

I hear her whispering in the dark, "I can't move my legs." Her eyes are wide and frightened as she reaches for the call light in her blue nightgown. "I can't move my legs," she reports to the person on the other end of the intercom. "I'll be right there," says the nameless voice. My vantage point is from the ceiling; I am looking down on her in her panic as she waits for the nurse.

Suddenly, I woke up drenched in sweat and breathing shallowly. I regained my bearings and felt the solidity of my bed beneath me. I was not in the hospital, not floating on the ceiling. I was in my own bed, wet now with my anxious sweat. It seemed so real. "Thank God," I whispered. "Thank God it was just a dream."

The next morning I made my daily sojourn to the hospital, where I would sit at her bedside as two different shifts of nurses made their rounds and carried out their care. I would see doctors, X-ray and blood technicians, respiratory therapists, dietary aides, and housekeeping staff come and go in the seemingly endless flow of personnel that moves through a hospital room on any given day. My mother and I would talk, laugh, cry, read, watch TV, eat terrible meals, nap, and visit with whichever of the *other siblings came that day. I would help her bathe, comb her hair (she really loved that, so I would take my time and turn this functional task into long, lovely, and tender pampering), change her colostomy bag, do Therapeutic Touch, and keep watch over her IV. The nurses, too few for the number of patients, would appreciate my care, too.*

I stepped off the elevator on the oncology floor and began the walk down the long carpeted corridor to her room. It's a strange thing: I could usually tell even before I got there what kind of a day it was, how things were going. I was feeling uneasy as I walked, and my pace quickened almost imperceptibly. I took a deep breath as I prepared to enter her room. Inside, seeing nothing obviously wrong, I began to relax. As was our routine by then, I gave her a kiss on the forehead and inquired about her night. Sitting up in the bed in her blue nightgown she gave me the report. I stood there in stunned silence, a shiver running down my spine. It had not been a dream. And it wouldn't be the last time that, while caring for her, I would experience an entirely new way of knowing and being.

I do not know why intimate involvement in the care of another should open one to such experiences. I only know that it does, both from my own experience and from the experiences that others have shared with me over the years. Perhaps this opening comes from the dropping of our defenses in the vulnerability of our shared suffering. Perhaps it is simply one of the hidden gifts, the unexpected rewards, for our offering of care.

I Am a Woman Achieving My Goals

I am an amazing, creative, competent, capable being and I can do whatever I decide to do. I have the vision to set goals for myself and all the talent and skill I need to meet them. I am resilient, persistent, tenacious, voracious, determined, and insistent. I have learned my lessons well; I pace myself realistically and I make sure I create downtime for rest and renewal. I know how to recognize my own fears and I know how to get myself through them. I can think clearly, decide firmly, and implement decisively. I am, after all, a woman; I can do hard things, especially hard things I have decided to do. I am a *woman achieving my goals.*

I Am a Woman Standing with All My Sisters

I have been guilty of violence to other women. When I have harshly judged women for making choices different from mine, I have been violent to women. When I have refused to speak up when someone is ridiculing another women in my presence, I have been violent to women. When I allowed a married man to have an intimate relationship with me, I was violent to women. When I laughed at sexist jokes, or criticized women for being too soft-minded rather than offering constructive feedback about the work (not the woman), I have been violent to women. These are not easy things to see in oneself, yet they have to be seen, have to be acknowledged, and then they have to be forgiven with a firm intention to stop the violence—not only because it is wrong to hurt other women, but also because in every one of these acts of violence toward other women there is an act of violence toward the womanself of the perpetrator. Violence against women stops with me. I am a *woman standing with all of my sisters.*

I Am a Woman Getting Out of My Own Way

*M*y instincts are almost always correct. My inner womanwisdom speaks to me, guiding me and leading me. When I follow, life flows. This book is my most recent example. As I was preparing for my first meeting with the woman who would become my editor, I compiled a summary of the books I thought I was qualified to write. Almost as an afterthought I placed in the folder a small leaflet of writing I had done eight years ago. It was a little book of ten affirmations of healing for women, all beginning with the stem, *I am a woman*. . . . As I placed it in my bag, I couldn't imagine showing it to her. It was a simple project, not anything like the more intellectual and academic texts I had in mind to produce. I almost didn't take it out of the bag at our meeting, but something in me insisted. Fortunately, I listened and stayed out of the way of what was trying to emerge.

I could have easily stopped the flow with overanalyzing, second-guessing, and doubt, all of which are forms of fear. I could have easily made my fear of looking simple and foolish more important than listening to and following my deep womanwisdom. Now I am more certain than ever. When I remind myself that there is a deep mystery that is unfolding through my life and that I cannot control it, only allow it, participate in it, trust it, be true to it, then I step back into the flow. I become fearless, at least in that moment, and I become a *woman getting out of my own way.*

I Am a Woman Fighting for What I Believe In

*A*n eighteen-year-old African-American high school senior became a heroine of mine in July 1996. Her name is Keshia Thomas. Keshia was part of a crowd of three hundred people assembled to protest a Ku Klux Klan rally in Ann Arbor, Michigan. A man who looked like a white supremacist was spotted in the protesters' midst, and there was suddenly an angry mob surrounding him. The crowd started beating him, knocking him to the pavement, and Keshia, who had been one of the people who was going to verbally confront him, threw herself on top of the man to protect him from the attack. The picture in the July 8 issue of *People* magazine of this young woman grimacing, using her body to protect the bald-headed, tattooed man as he lay on the ground is etched in my memory, as is Keshia's explanation of what she did. Keshia's was decidedly a woman's act of courage. She was there in the first place to stand against violence and oppression. And when she actually witnessed them, it was the feminine voice that arose, fearless, strong, powerful, in protection of all life. "You don't beat a man up because he doesn't believe the same things you do. He's still somebody's child," she said. Then she laughingly told the *People* reporter that "this will all be over in a New York minute. People don't have to remember my name. I just want them to remember that I did the right thing." I remember both, Keshia, and you give me the courage to be a ***woman fighting for what I believe in.***

A Reflection: ON RECLAIMING MY SPIRITUAL HOME

*T*o be fair, I must admit that the priest presiding at my mother's 1978 funeral had never met her, never even set eyes on her as part of the faithful congregation assembled each Sunday. For reasons that we never talked about, though I suspect were related to birth control, my mother was not a practicing Catholic. Even as she was dying, she did not ask for a priest, and I, a lapsed Catholic myself, didn't suggest one. Nevertheless, she did want burial from the church, and so I arranged for a funeral mass in what would have been her parish, had she ever joined.

As the service began out in the gathering space of the church, the presiding priest began to read from a book of prayers to bless my mother's coffin. As he read quickly and in English that was barely understandable to me, he came to a place in the passage marked N———, into which he would (presumably seamlessly) insert the name of the deceased as he continued reading. However, such was not the way this particular blessing proceeded. "What's his name?" the priest queried to no one in particular and without looking up from the book. "Her name was Georgia," I replied. He continued, reaching the next N———, and, unbelievably, repeated his previous question, no gender correction added. This debacle concluded, we proceeded into the church.

Gathered in the pews were employees from all of the branches of the bank for which my mother was a branch manager. It was a large turnout, which we did not expect and which was very touching to my siblings and me. The priest gave a predictably generic sermon, given that he did not know the woman for whom this funeral mass was being offered. This was fine. What was not fine was his condemnation of anyone who died outside of the Catholic faith. "Today is a great celebration for George," he intoned, "because he is in heaven now. Do not weep! But weep for all the pagans who die every day who will burn in the fires of hell for all eternity!" I will spare you the rest of the details—you get the picture. I had no idea how many of the assembled mourners were "pagans," nor did I care, but he should have, I reasoned, and then and there, I quit. My gentle slide away from the Catholic church became an outright rejection. I would never go back.

And I didn't. Not for about ten years. Not until the day when I found myself inwardly compelled to open the doors of a tiny beach church on an island off the coast of South Carolina. I was staying on the island for the summer doing research with a colleague at the university there. I passed the little church each morning on a bike ride before work, but on this day, I simply couldn't continue on without stopping. The inner attraction to that church and what lay beyond its doors became overwhelming; I had to yield. I was not happy. In fact, I was terrified. Because as well as I could tell, it was Christ himself drawing me, and this, as anyone knows, is crazy.

What was happening to me wasn't crazy, but was an intense conversion experience that continued for many weeks. The end result, after the initial intensity and several years of processing lots of anger and resistance, is that I am now what I call a recycled Catholic. Some people find this phrase flip or even derogatory, but I love it. Recycling is about retaining the essence of something while discarding what is no longer useable. It is about a new form emerging from the remains of an old one. And perhaps what I like best about the metaphor is the transformative action at the heart of it. Recycling requires that there be some force applied to effect change, some energy which will literally pulverize an object so as to allow a new creation to emerge. In the recycling of objects, this force is physical or chemical. In the recycling of one's religious identity, this force is spiritual, but no less powerful. It has changed everything. Thankfully, everything.

I once told a spiritual director that "I'm not interested in being a good Catholic. I am interested in being faithful to the journey." This, I think, sums up the new form that has emerged from recycling. I have been called to be a disciple of Christ. The church is no longer my final authority, but a sacred vessel that provides sanctuary, support, and community for my journey. There are many who have gone before me to guide the way: extraordinary lovers of God such as Hildegard of Bingen and Julian of Norwich and Saint Francis of Assisi. There are beautiful, ancient traditions within my spiritual home that help to direct me on my path; there is a contemplative tradition; a mystical tradition; a healing tradition. The hosts of heaven and the communion of saints encircle me; the old rituals are new with mystical insights and provide deep soul nourishment. And while this church, this home, is an imperfect vessel, broken in many places and groaning for change, I am an imperfect pilgrim with brokenness and groanings of my own. It is, I think, a good fit.

I Am a Woman Having a Daring Adventure

*H*elen Keller wrote that life is either a daring adventure or nothing. I used to think this meant that if one wanted to be really alive, one should be doing things which defied death or risked some terrible harm to life and limb. In other words, that a daring adventure is defined by the physical riskiness of the activities. But now I know better. Now I see that just staying alive and thriving from day to day is an adventure! When I think about the whole of life as a daring adventure to be embraced, enjoyed, and learned from instead of a series of hurdles to get over and stresses to avoid or to recover from, I become less afraid, less protective and constricted.

One of my daily adventures is meditation. This, to most, might not seem very adventurous. Yet when one realizes that meditation is, finally, about union with Ultimate Reality, whatever name one wishes to use, it's hard to think of anything more adventurous—or dangerous, if you want to know the truth. But there I am, just sitting on a pillow as still as a shadow.

Some adventures turn out better than others. Several months ago I was the guest teacher in a class at the university, where I hadn't been for many months. I was anxious and tense, but was only mildly aware of it. The focus of the class was creating a community of caring. Somehow, in the course of the first half hour of our time together, I had lost it with first one, and then a pair of students. I challenged them in a very direct and strong way, hardly creating a sense of caring or community. In other words, I blew it.

I quickly noticed what had happened and I took responsibility for it with the class. I told them about my anxiety and I apologized to the students, trying to model both self-awareness and self-responsibility. One of the students never looked at me and refused my apology at the break. I felt sad, but satisfied that I had done the best I could do in this daring adventure of teaching a new class and showing up as a whole, imperfect, but honest human being.

When things don't go the way I would like, I remind myself that adventures are like that—you never know what's going to happen next. That's what makes them adventures. And with a little time out for wound care, I go on, ready to participate fully in the unfolding mystery, the great daring adventure of my life. I am a *woman having a daring adventure.*

I Am a Woman Working Without Hurry

When I was growing up in Brooklyn, there was a needlepoint sampler hanging in my neighbor's kitchen that said, "The hurrier I go, the behinder I get." I never really understood what it meant—not to mention that I was pretty sure the grammar was off. Now I see the simple truth of it. When I hurry the work I'm doing I feel anxious, worried, and tense. These feelings distort my view of everything else. I get completely overwhelmed. Will I ever catch up? This attitude creates the perfect conditions for making mistakes, as I learned long ago with one of my first patients.

I was behind schedule. I quickly read the doctor's orders for my postoperative patient and proceeded directly to his room, scissors drawn. "Good news," I announced, waving my scissors, and without hesitation smoothly removed his urinary catheter, much to his delight. I walked down the hall wheeling the IV pole, which held the irrigating solution that had been running through my patient's bladder, along with the rubber tube I had removed. The head nurse looked up from the desk and spotted me. "What is that?" she asked me. "The discontinued catheter from my patient in room 409," I said quickly, eager to get on with my next task. "You removed his catheter?" she exclaimed, and I began to get the idea that something was wrong. "Read this," she commanded as she opened the doctor's order book. I reread the order and turned white. The order was to discontinue the irrigation, not the catheter. The patient would have to be recatheterized, which would not be pleasant for him.

I sat at the patient's bedside and cried as I told him and apologized profusely. A gentle and kind man, he put an arm around me and told me that nobody is perfect and that he would be all right. And although I was grateful for his forgiveness, I felt even worse that such a wonderful person was being caused needless discomfort.

It was a powerful lesson, all those years ago. Yet some lessons take a lifetime to integrate. I still have a tendency to rush when I feel behind. But I can usually catch myself before it gets too out of hand. I know that if I can stop at that moment, take a long, deep breath, center myself, and bring my full awareness into the present moment, the work actually goes faster, my ordering of priorities becomes clearer, and I have a much better time. Productivity goes up and stress comes down when I am a *woman working without hurry.*

A Reflection: ON THE CONSCIOUS CHOICE TO CARE

*A*s I cross the threshold into the medical ICU, I sustain a direct attack on my senses. Sights, sounds, smells, and sensations threaten to overwhelm me. I feel myself step back, but my body is frozen and does not move. The step is internal. I am like a flower at sunset, petals coming together to protect the delicate center from the chill of night. Gathered into itself, it rests, until the sunlight coaxes unfolding once again.

Here in the ICU, the sun doesn't shine. Without sunlight the flower will eventually die, as will the nurse. So choices will have to be made along the way. Sometimes, when it seems safe enough, or when she can't help it, she will open. She will be there, her delicate and tender center exposed and defenseless. It will usually be in direct response to the need in someone's eyes. It may be fear, panic, loneliness, despair, or pain. When the eyes of another person, maybe too weak to speak, maybe paralyzed, maybe on the ventilator, look into the eyes of the nurse, when they are wide with pleading—*I need you. I need a real live human being. I am afraid. Are you there? Do you see me?*—that she cannot resist.

She is, after all, really a nurse. And so in those brief and fleeting moments, often in the middle of the night, she turns toward the sun, opening to the radiance of a fully present encounter with the spirit of another human being. Being present to people at the most vulnerable and frightening times in their lives is, of course, why she became a nurse, but it is always dangerous, always carries with it the risks that accompany direct contact with the depths of human anguish, suffering, and torment.

The raw truth of these encounters can inspire, energize, and create awe. But it can also consume one in the literal fires of hell, leaving one with wounds that weep, like the drainage from a bad burn. Such are the realities of the decision to care. Some find a way to heal the wounds and keep meeting people in the often brutal truth of their lives. They find sustenance outside of the unit, or develop some way of coping that sustains them in this sacred healing work.

The tragic ones are those who shut down but stay anyway. They are competent and they are efficient. But when the patient looks into the eyes of these nurses for some sign that he still exists as a person, even though he cannot move a muscle, cannot breathe alone, or reach out a hand or even cry, he will not find it.

I take a deep breath and consciously expand from the inside out. I pray that Spirit will guide me; that I may stay alive here, open and ready to say with eyes and voice and touch and energy, "Yes, yes, I am here; it's okay; I see you; it's all right; you are not alone; I am your nurse; I am with you." Slowly, I continue my walk into the unit to begin my shift.

I Am a Woman Choosing Bliss

*W*hen I awake in the morning and step solidly onto my previously broken ankle, walking easily and painlessly from my bed into my day, I feel blissful. When I am flying west at sunset, escorted home by brilliant colors and spectacular light that keep unfolding into more and more unspeakable beauty, I am in bliss, full of awe and gratitude. Bliss, I have learned, is not something I have to wait for. Bliss is available to me, here and now, today, in the very circumstances of my unique life, in this very moment. It doesn't matter what the circumstances are; what matters is that I take the time to notice life unfolding in every breath.

In my very next breath I can choose to open and allow bliss to fill me. I can choose to center myself in inner stillness and connect with infinite Source, infinite light, infinite love. I can breathe deeply of all the good and the blessings that are intended for me, gifts from Creation, free and priceless. I can remember in that instant all the people who care for me and can expand into their love. I can choose to notice the exquisite ease with which breath enters and leaves my body, 28,800 times a day. Each exhalation, a letting go; each inhalation, a new beginning; 28,800 chances a day to choose again. I am a ***woman choosing bliss.***

I Am a Woman Giving Myself a Break

I have said, "Give yourself a break," to so many people in my life—friends, colleagues, clients, family members. But so often I forget to take my own advice. A friend and I laugh because we each do the same thing—there can be 799 glowing evaluations of a speech we gave that was followed by a standing ovation, but we will focus on the one evaluation that says something snide or derogatory and we will ruin our pleasure. Sometimes I am my worst critic, my internal voice mercilessly judging me about everything from what I look like to how well I give a talk.

I ruin my pleasure in other ways, too, like not listening to my bodymind when it says *enough* of sitting and thinking and tapping away at the computer—get up! Move! Take a walk with your puppy! Soak in a hot bubble bath! When I don't listen, I ruin the pleasure of my work by overdoing it and I deny my body-mind of the pleasures it longs for. So, right now and whenever I start criticizing myself, I need to become a *woman giving myself a break.*

I Am a Woman Who Has Proved I Can Do It

I have made it in the world. I can talk the language, write the words, reason and analyze, hypothesize and generalize. I can commute, compute, stress out, and eat in. I can live on adrenaline and relax with a cocktail. I can be reached at any time, day or night, by fax, cell phone, or pager. I have a platinum charge card, premier executive boarding privileges, and a membership in the Red Carpet Club. I can hire and I can fire; I can give raises and I can cut spending. I can spend most of my days in a room with glass walls called windows (why?) breathing the same air over and over and not even notice. I can come home exhausted, eat a TV dinner, collapse, and get up tomorrow to do it all over again. I can do it! And now that I know that, I can seriously ask myself the next question—do I really want to? I am a *woman who has proved I can do it.*

I Am a Woman Centered
in the Present Moment

*T*he present moment is the only true place of power in my life. It is the singular container for my life experience, the sole possibility for my action in the world, the lone opportunity to create something new, different, true. When I allow myself to spend excessive amounts of time ruminating, regretting, or rehashing some event or interaction from the past, I'm missing my life as it is unfolding here and now in the present moment. When I allow myself to be drawn, over and over, into idle fantasies about future scenarios, or into worrying and fretting about things that may never happen, I am missing the precious opportunity to create actions now that will determine my future. Processing of past events is important to me, and then I return to the now. Planning what I can for the future is responsible of me, then I return to the now. To truly live a life that's mine, to create a life of my own choosing, I have to show up in the present, not stay lost in the past or be transported into the future. I am a *woman centered in the present moment.*

A Reflection: ON HONORING RETURNING MOTHERS

A friend I hadn't seen for several years came up to me at a conference, and we started playing catch-up. She is a gifted psychotherapist and has had a thriving private practice for years. As we stood in the hallway amid the comings and goings of other conference attendees, she shared her news with me. She had closed her practice because, as she put it, "My children need me at home."

I heard in her voice her clarity, her certainty, her power, and her love, all at the same time. She was not forced, but free. She was not admitting defeat; she was claiming her right to choose. Somehow I felt her fierce and tender mothersoul there, and it touched me, moved me to tears right there in the busy corridor. I embraced her. "I honor you, my friend, I honor your decision to be there with your children. I am in awe of your courage and your strength. You inspire me."

A few weeks later I received a card which contained these words: "The transition from a habit of 'doing' to a life that embraces 'being' with my-self and my children is the most empowering act I've taken in my life. Yet, feelings of insecurity still hover. Thank you for your reverent recognition of this recent life change; it felt very validating." On the bottom of the card was pasted a little cloth cutout of a smiling doll cartoon and on the envelope, a cloth cutout of a flower. Gifts from my sister, a mother at home, tending, nurturing, and being. The feminine soul free and unin-hibited. Such sweetness for us all. So much delight to support and honor each other's choices, each other's work, each other's lives. We all stand in one enormous circle, and knowing that every woman who finds her own true voice, her own authentic path, strengthens the whole circle, we sup-port each other, encourage each other, embrace each other, help each other. When our women's circle grows strong enough, we will be able to lift up the world.

I Am a Woman Becoming My Best Self

I have had glimpses of a deep self. It is light and free, easy with the faults of others and with my own human weakness. This self is patient and kind, generous and gentle. This self is always at peace, always in love, even when people and situations are difficult. This self is so full it seeks only to give itself away in a grateful outpouring of its heart's content. I have seen this self, tasted her joy, bathed in the inner warmth of her beauty, smelled the perfume of a self temporarily selfless. I have collapsed to my knees in gratitude at having been given the chance to see, even momentarily, where Spirit is leading me, what God is making of me, deep below my conscious mind, deep within the secret womb of my womansoul. Some days I feel far from that self. I see only my weaknesses, my smallnesses, my little ego attachments and power struggles. At these times when I want to give up on myself, the glimpse of something deeper is an answer to prayer, assuring me that I am not alone, and that I am loved now, as well as I will be later, when Spirit is finished with me. Because I have glimpsed what is possible, I surrender and trust that, through my efforts supported by the pure gift of grace, I am a *woman becoming my best self.*

I Am a Woman Freeing Others
from My Resentment

I did not speak to my father for ten of the last twelve or thirteen years. Something happened, we argued, and I withdrew. Further fueled with my rage about some painful aspects of my childhood, I felt fully justified in my resentment and in my refusal to have anything more to do with him. Each Christmas, as the family gathered at my sister's house, there was the same dance. He would call, or my sister would call him. One by one, everyone would get on the phone for Christmas greetings. I would disappear. "No," they would say, "I don't know where she went off to." But, of course, they did. Every year, for ten years, I ate Christmas dinner with a knot in my belly, because I knew that sooner or later the phone call would come. If the phone rang, I was already on my feet, ready to flee, adrenaline pumping. All of this, I assumed, was punishing him—*him!* How blind and foolish and sad.

I might have continued this way forever except for one small problem. I was a teacher and a practitioner of healing. I was seriously engaged in prayer and meditation as a way of life. I had made a deep, inner commitment to live my life as an instrument of love, and, failing that, to at least do no harm. This treatment of my father, no matter how justified I felt, was out of integrity with my life path and my soul's deepest values. I knew I was causing him pain and suffering. I was up against a wall.

I did the only thing I knew how to do—I prayed for years that someday God would help me to forgive him. I didn't realize that my prayers were answered until, astonished, I found myself standing in front of the Easter cards looking at the ones addressed to fathers. Easter. New beginnings; new life after death; the return of what was once lost. I sent my father an Easter card. Over the following days I noticed that I was happier, easier, more relaxed, and more alive than I had felt in a long time. Most meaningful of all was the deep sense of peace and rightness I felt within. By releasing my father from my resentment, I had freed myself.

Resentment is energy, just like love. The feel of resentment in my body is tight, constricting, heavy, and tense. It feels oppressive and hopeless. In the past I've made the mistake of thinking that these miserable feelings are the fault of the people I resent—if they hadn't hurt me, disappointed me, used me, abused me, I wouldn't be resentful and I'd feel better. But that isn't true, and when I stay stuck in that thinking, I give away my power. I let the behavior of other people determine how I feel. Also I don't give God any opening in which to work on my behalf. I want more love in my life and less resentment, and the only person who can accomplish that is me, with the help and guidance of Spirit. When I release other people from my resentment, I release myself into the energy of love, which feels open, light, and free in my body. It's my choice, and I choose to be a *woman freeing others from my resentment.*

I Am a Woman Owning My Power

I am a powerful woman! I am strong and clear in my intentions, capable in my actions, creative in my choices, astute in my observations, wise in my judgments. I know what is right and I know what is not right for me and for those for whom I care. When I discern right action, I act deliberately and use the full power of all that I have become to make a difference in life. I do not measure my success by the size of the change. Some women create national organizations or run for Congress. Others make sure that stop signs go up where they are needed or take in homeless teenagers until they can get relocated. Each of us is called to use her power in ways that are particular to our own lives. Each time we heed the call, we join with all women who use their power to create a better world. I choose to be among them. I choose to be a *woman owning my power.*

I Am a Woman Using My Voice
to Create Change

*R*aising my voice, if that is what it takes to be heard, is not being a hysterical female. Declaring my anger without apology is not being a bitchy female. Allowing myself to feel my rage when I am confronted with abuses of power that reduce human beings to things, I am not being a bleeding heart. Well, actually I am being a bleeding heart and I freely choose to let my heart be wounded by such outrageous behavior. I am a woman who seeks to see and tell the truth. I am a woman who seeks to speak from my center and to name what I see in the service of healing, in the service of life, in the service of love. I am a woman who has experienced the power of words and language to tear down and diminish or to build up and honor. I am a woman who struggles to use language as a vehicle for both; for tearing down what separates us, and for building up what unites us; for diminishing our fears of each other, and for honoring the holy mystery that is each unique person. Using language clearly and forcefully is one of the ways in which I become more powerful. It is my right, and I will no longer be intimidated by the voices of others who seek to silence me. I am a *woman using my voice to create change.*

A few weeks ago I gave a speech that was very well received. Many people came up to me throughout the day, thanking me with hugs and handshakes and broad smiles and tears in their eyes. I made a conscious choice to receive from these sisters and brothers; to take in the outpouring of love that they were offering me; to allow their love to nourish me. With each person, I looked into her eyes and breathed in what she was offering as if it were the fragrance of spring lilacs or summer roses. I opened my heart and let the breath flow downward, bathing me in sweet delight. I left the conference glowing and floating, in bliss, really, full of love and appreciation. And I smiled at everyone I met as I shopped for dinner. Love flows outward.

I have been giving speeches almost all my life, it seems. What made this scenario different was my attitude. I am not used to actually taking in praise and love. In quite an unconscious way, I usually see the time after a speech as an opportunity to give more to people—to meet them with love and caring, me to them—because I'm the speaker/giver and they are the listeners/receivers. I am the teacher and they are the students. I am the nurse, and they are the patients. I am the older sister, and they are the younger siblings. It has always seemed quite natural, quite the way things ought to be.

But it is not quite natural and it isn't the way things ought to be at all. On the surface, it's clear that one needs to take in energy to keep giving it out. I typically count on God alone as my energy source, which, on first glance, doesn't seem like a bad idea. And it's not a bad idea, just an incomplete one, with an incomplete idea of who and where God is, and how God supports us. And—here is the arrogance of it—disguised as simple caring, my refusal to let other people be one of God's ways of nourishing me allows me to maintain a position of control and nonvulnerability with other human beings. What looks like a great spiritual ideal is really a cop-out on real, authentic, embodied interdependence. I hate vulnerability, I discovered when I did a little looking.

I discovered a few other things while I rummaged through my old baggage, such as the fact that when I maintain this position, which I am now calling the saint stance toward life, I deny other people the right to receive the same joy from giving that I receive. This saintly posture says, essentially, that I'm only too happy to allow your vulnerability, to allow you to receive love through me but, thank you, I really don't need love from you. The person may not even realize consciously that her gift, so full of tenderness and authentic care, has been refused, but her soul knows. The soul always knows when it has been welcomed and when it has been refused entry. When we refuse the gift of each other's caring, we chip away at the soul's willingness to risk itself again, and this is not okay—because we need more risking, more caring, more loving, more supporting, more affirming, more tenderness, more nurturing, more love in our world, not less.

Letting myself be loved is at least as much a service to the people I engage with as loving them, and maybe even more so, because when I allow myself to be loved, to receive their gift, I become vulnerable to them. And there is little else we can give each other that is more precious than an undefended self, a self open and receptive, a self that can admit need, admit longing, admit how absolutely fantastic it feels to be loved. It is the feminine at its very strongest, its most sacred. And it heals all of us.

I Am a Woman Letting Go and Moving On

*L*ife is change. It's the one thing we can be sure of, but often it's the one thing we fight against the most. As I get older, I am beginning to see that I create pain and struggle in my life by my refusal to change. This frightened clinging has destructive effects not only for me, but for those who are in my life. I keep us all stuck in habits and patterns that don't serve us, because what I know is always less frightening than what I don't know—even if what I know is that the present isn't working!

I recently began a new project that involves working with a team, instead of on my own, to teach a workshop. The class is based on my work, but because there will now be others involved, it won't be taught the way I have always done. At our first meeting together, I noticed myself feeling tense and irritated. But rather than simply suffering in silence or arguing for my way of doing the course, I practiced letting go. I took several deep breaths. I listened quietly to what the others were actually saying rather than what I thought they might be saying, which was that my way of doing it wasn't good enough. I took more deep breaths. And then I reminded myself that the only thing happening here was change; something new was trying to emerge. Then I began to feel a little twinge of excitement bubbling up. I realized that maybe I would really like having other people share the burden of course development and teaching, instead of my carrying it all alone. I joined in the discussion of this new, joint venture.

This is not a huge change in my life; not, for example, a serious illness or the loss of a loved one. But it is change nevertheless, and it is practice in letting go for the larger changes that life will inevitably ask of me.

Refusing to let go and allow life to flow and change exhausts me and prevents me from using my energy to respond to new challenges creatively. Staying stuck in asking "Why me?" or in blaming others for my new circumstances prevents me from finding new solutions. Most of all, trying to hold on to the past is as useless as trying to keep the sea from ebbing after high tide and just as joyless. I want joy and happiness to be the foundation of my life. I am in charge of this; no one else, just me. I know now that my best opportunity for creating a joyful life when life asks me to change is to be a *woman letting go and moving on.*

I Am a Woman Dreaming a New Dream

*D*reams live inside all of us. Daydreams or night dreams inspire us, comfort us, give us direction and purpose. Dreams tell us something about what is really important to us, what we most care about, what we most desire. Sometimes life brings us exactly what we have been dreaming of. But sometimes life shatters our dreams, shredding them to pieces and throwing them onto the fires of our suffering. This doesn't mean that our dreams were wrong or that we shouldn't dream again. It means that what was true at one time is no longer. It means that life has called us to let go of that dream, to surrender to the truth of what is happening now, and in that surrendering, to begin to grow beyond what we have been able to imagine for ourselves. Only if we can let go of dreams that are no longer real, that no longer serve us, can we open fully to the present and let ourselves begin again. Out of our surrender, out of our willingness to accept the present reality and our lost dream will come something new. We make a space to become a *woman dreaming a new dream.*

I Am a Woman Rejoicing in Sisterhood

*M*y sister and I are as different as any two people can be, at least that's the way I see it. No one can make me more angry more quickly than she. But then again, no one makes me laugh harder or adores me more. I don't know if we ever would have picked each other as friends, or if we had, if our friendship would have survived. It doesn't matter. Sisters are different from friends—they're tribal kin, and in the best possible way you are stuck with each other for life, whether you're good or bad, naughty or nice. Even when contact becomes erratic or stops for periods of time, final withdrawal from the relationship isn't an option. You're together; you just are—joyfully, thankfully, loyally, furiously, truthfully, painfully, playfully, dependably together on this road called life. And no matter what has transpired between you during the months or days before you need her, when you need a sister, your sis is there. That's how it is in a tribe. I am a ***woman rejoicing in sisterhood.***

I Am a Woman Respecting Myself

Respect—re-spect—means to look again. I am a woman looking again at myself and liking what I see. I am doing the very best I can with the resources and gifts I have been given. I am staying on my path, fulfilling my responsibilities. I deserve respect, not for anything I've done, but for the simple reason that I am a human being. Whether my work in the world is cleaning the executive bathroom or being the sole owner of its key has no bearing here—I deserve no more or no less respect because of my work. Respect is my birthright. But respect begins with me. For too long I have allowed others to determine my opinion of myself. Somewhere I heard the phrase, your opinion of me is none of my business. It's true, but I haven't always acted that way. I have allowed others' ideas about my ideas and about women to make me feel embarrassed, humiliated, and foolish, losing respect for myself. That was then, and this is now. Now, I am a *woman respecting myself.*

EPILOGUE:

ON WOMEN'S BUSINESS

In an earlier reflection (page 81) I told the story of the young boy I met on an airplane who was crying because he had to leave his mother to return to his father's home. There is more to that story. When the flight arrived, I was one of the first to leave the aircraft. He had to wait until everyone else was off the plane for the flight attendant to accompany him down the jetway. I wanted to see my young friend's father. I don't really know why; somehow I just wanted to see their reunion, perhaps hopeful that I would see some joy in it, some redemption. I waited at a newsstand quite a way from the gate for them to pass.

When they finally arrived in sight, I literally felt sick. The tiny boy, head lowered, carrying his bunny and his little backpack, was trailing several feet behind his father, who was marching straight ahead. The first wave of gut reaction was quickly followed by the welling up of a fierce rage. In that moment I wanted to pounce on that man like a mother lion and nail him to the ground with my hands around his throat. I wanted to roar in his ears, "LOOK! Look at what you are doing! Look at him—do you see him? Do you know what he is going through? Do you care?" I barely kept myself from moving—barely—and struggled to take a deep breath as they slipped from my line of vision.

I quickly invented a litany of reasons why what I had seen probably wasn't what it seemed. I told myself that maybe the father had tried to hold the hand of the boy, but he had refused. Or maybe the father had put the boy down from his embrace and the boy fell behind just in the very moment I witnessed. Or maybe the boy had just said, "I hate you," and the father was hurt, trying to recover his poise so he could return to the boy's side. Maybe he was just having a bad day. It's not my business to judge him or to interfere, I told myself. Not my business to tell someone how to act with his child. I sadly and slowly moved on through the terminal, still feeling slightly ill.

In another time and place there is another story. I had returned to my car after doing some shopping. As I turned to pull my seatbelt from its holder, I noticed a pair of little eyes looking at me from within the car parked to my left. Below the little eyes were a button nose and a friendly smile greeting me, all of which belonged to a blond-haired girl no more than six years old. In the back was a toddler in a car seat who was sitting quite still. As I looked, I realized that both of the children had very red faces. It was a hot day, and all the windows of the car were closed.

I remembered a news story of a baby left alone in a car who died from the heat and I became worried. Noticing that the car was an older model, I was hopeful that it had manually controlled windows. I motioned to the little one in the passenger seat to roll down her window. She was hesitant, following instructions, I thought to myself, for her safety. Yet it was that very safety I was concerned about. I motioned to put the window down just a "teensy bit, to get some air," I said loudly so she could hear me through the door. She finally agreed, rolled down the window, and we chatted a bit.

I did not want to leave the two children alone with the window down, and so I decided to wait until the adult returned. He did in about five minutes. I got out of my car as he was loading his purchases into the trunk of his. "You know," I said, with as much gentleness as I could, "it's a very hot day, and these children are very young. Do you think it was such a good idea to leave them alone in a locked car?" He ignored me. I repeated my query. He told me angrily to mind my own business. I said that that was exactly what I was doing, and that if I didn't hear a better answer than that from him, I would report him to Social Services, since leaving young children in a car unattended is considered neglect in this country. He gave me the finger and drove off. I went home and made the phone call, but the Department of Social Services said that it probably would not investigate because it did not have enough personnel.

The difference between the first and the second story is that by the time the second incident had occurred, I had come to a new understanding of just what "my business" is. My business is women's business. My business is tending, nurturing, loving, and caring for life in all its forms, but most especially in the form of those who cannot fend for themselves. My business is to keep noticing when a child is being hurt, or neglected, or when women are being abused, diminished, demeaned. My business is to be fiercely willing to name these things and to do what I can to change them. My business is to use my voice to speak out, in person, in the moment, naming what is wrong with the act I am seeing, but with love and care and tenderness for the person committing the act.

I may anger some people. I may hurt the feelings of some well-intentioned, harried parents who are doing the very best they can. This is not my intention. This is why I must be willing to be gentle in my approach, bringing an open heart, love, and compassion as companions to my fierceness. I might even volunteer to sit with the children while the parent finishes some necessary task—and to give them my driver's license or my wallet, if that's what it takes, to help them feel safe about it.

Finally, it is equally important that I know what really is none of my business. My business is not what happens after I act; it is not making sure that the world is different because of my voice. To see change in the world as the measure of my value is to doom myself to a relentless sense of failure, because it is never enough; there is always another child, another woman, more violence, more poverty. It is my business to do what I am uniquely called to do as woman—to bring as much love, kindness, nurturing, caring, and healing as I can muster into this world; in my own home and in the supermarket; on airplanes and in parking lots; in classrooms and hospitals, boardrooms and Laundromats; on podiums and through national television; across my back fence or halfway across the globe. It is God's business to use these acts to change the world. We are a very good team. I am a woman finding my voice.

Dear Reader,
The following pages have been provided to inspire you in finding *your* voice. I invite you to send me any meditations or reflections that you write for possible inclusion in a second book on this theme. Please include all the means of communicating with you, including E-mail and fax numbers. I can't respond to or return submissions, but if we decide to include yours in the book, we will be in touch with you.

Janet F. Quinn, Ph.D., R.N.
HaelanWorks
3080 Third Street
Boulder, CO 80304
Fax: (303) 449-2584
E-mail: womanvoice@aol.com

I am a woman...

I am a woman...

I am a woman...

A Reflection on...

A Reflection on...

A Reflection on...